Running around in circles

Coordinating childcare, education and work

Christine Skinner

The POLICY

PP

PRESS

First published in Great Britain in May 2003 by

The Policy Press
University of Bristol
Fourth Floor, Beacon House
Queen's Road
Bristol BS8 1QU
UK

Tel no +44 (0)117 331 4054
Fax no +44 (0)117 331 4093
E-mail tpp-info@bristol.ac.uk
www.policypress.org.uk

Published for the Joseph Rowntree Foundation by The Policy Press

British Library Cataloguing in Publication Data
A catalogue record for this book is available from the British Library.

Library of Congress Cataloging-in-Publication Data
A catalog record for this book has been requested.

ISBN 1 86134 466 X

Christine Skinner is Lecturer in Social Policy in the Department of Social Policy and Social Work, University of York.

The **Joseph Rowntree Foundation** has supported this project as part of its programme of research and innovative development projects, which it hopes will be of value to policy makers, practitioners and service users. The facts presented and views expressed in this report are, however, those of the author and not necessarily those of the Foundation.

Cover design by Qube Design Associates, Bristol
Printed in Great Britain by Hobbs the Printers Ltd, Southampton

Contents

List of tables and figures

Tables

Figures

Acknowledgements

This report was based on data originally
collected for a European study exploring the
reconciliation of work and family life across five
EU countries. The study originated at Roskilde
University and was financed by the Danish Social
Science Research Council and the universities of
Copenhagen, Umeå and Roskilde. My special
thanks go to the director of the UK part of the
project, Professor Peter Abrahamson, for his
permission to analyse the UK data in depth for
this report. I would also like to thank the Joseph
Rowntree Foundation Advisory Group members:
Barbara Ballard, Professor Shirley Dex, Professor
Jonathan Bradshaw, Jane Costello, Jo Armistead,
Lynn Richards and Liz Haigh. My gratitude also
goes to Professor Janet Ford for comments on an
early draft and to Mr Pat Thornton for his help
with the graphics. Most importantly, I thank the
40 respondents in England who took part in the
original study.

Coordinating childcare and educational needs with employment arrangements

This report examines the experiences of 40 English mothers in coordinating childcare and paid work commitments within the context of women's increased labour market participation. It is based on a qualitative study involving mothers who live in a specific locality and it provides an in-depth analysis from a 'family unit' perspective, that is, exploring what mothers and fathers do to manage the needs of *all* the children in the family. A great deal is known about childcare arrangements for children of different ages, but little is known about how parents with more than one child coordinate childcare and education with work commitments. Formal childcare, pre-school and school education is generally provided in separate institutional settings in the UK. Crucially, these different settings have to be temporally, spatially and physically managed by parents and children, and there is evidence to suggest that these are not trivial barriers to women's access to paid employment (Ungerson and Kember, 1997). Thus, managing paid work and childcare involves more than just a temporal exercise in juggling different family members' needs and preferences (Ungerson and Kember, 1997; Glover, 1998). It also involves coordinating the different types of service provision attached to individual children alongside work commitments, a process that can become even more complex in the context of non-standard working hours and flexible work arrangements (Perrons and Hurstfield, 1998).

Within the context of policy driving women's increased labour market participation, it is therefore important to understand more about how parents actually manage childcare/education and paid work and what factors facilitate or hinder coordination, including how this might vary by socioeconomic status. This study provides rich information on the routines operated by parents in their everyday lives, the strategies they used to successfully coordinate the childcare and educational needs of children alongside work commitments and it provides some useful insights into how coordination factors can act as a barrier to women's employment.

Background

The last decade has shown a consistent rise in the number of mothers with dependent children[1] entering the labour market, up from 59% in 1991 to 65% in 2001. Most mothers are in part-time (60%) rather than full-time work (40%) and the employment rate varies by the age of the youngest child. In spring 2001, where the youngest child was five years old or less, the participation rate was lowest at 54%[2]. This rose consecutively to 70% and 75% where the youngest child was aged between 5 and 10 years (primary school age) or aged between 11 and 15 (Twomey, 2002, p 121). However, evidence suggests that there is no consistent sudden jump when the youngest child reaches school age (Paull and Taylor, 2002). Mothers are also returning to work earlier following the birth of a child: in 1979 less than a quarter of mothers returned to work within 9-11 months of giving

---

[1] Dependent children are defined as aged between 0 and 18 years (Twomey, 2002).

[2] This group of mothers showed the biggest rise in employment participation across the decade, up 11% from 1991.

birth; in 1997 this had increased to two thirds (NCOPF, 2002). Overall, therefore, more mothers are in paid work and more are working when their children are young. Alongside this, the nature of work itself has also changed.

Since the 1970s the labour market has been restructured, producing a decline in manufacturing and an increase in service sector jobs, many of which are held by women (Dex, 1999). Correspondingly, flexible jobs such as part-time working, self-employment and temporary contracts have increased and more people also work in the evenings and at weekends. In particular, mothers with dependent children are more likely to work evenings and weekends as they structure their hours around childcare requirements (partners providing free care at these times) (Dex, 1999). Some employers also offer 'family-friendly' work arrangements enabling parents to opt for part-time hours, flexitime arrangements and, less commonly, for term-time hours and working from home (Dex and Smith, 2002). A recent survey shows that nearly a quarter of employed parents have some choice over their hours of work with flexitime arrangements and the majority of employers say they would allow employees to vary their hours of work occasionally (Hogarth et al, 2000). Parents and especially mothers welcome this flexibility.

The changes in mothers' employment and the labour market mean that families have to increasingly find childcare to cover parents' and particularly mothers' working hours. Having access to appropriate childcare services is therefore a vital component of reconciling work and family life. Indeed, much has been done to improve childcare services (discussed later), but it is known that mothers and particularly lone mothers, still face significant barriers in returning to work as a result of a lack of good quality, convenient and affordable formal childcare (Bryson et al, 1999; Callender, 2000; Finch and Gloyer, 2000; La Valle et al, 2000; Childcare Commission Report, 2001; Strategy Unit, 2002; Woodland et al, 2002). Callender's (2000) survey shows that the supply of places does not meet demand and the Strategy Unit (2002, p 8) acknowledges there are shortages in most childcare markets. The Daycare Trust has argued that there are insufficient places for children less than three years old, for parents who work shifts or outside normal hours and for ethnic minority

groups (Daycare Trust, 2001). Other evidence on childcare outside normal hours suggests that, although there is a low demand from parents, providers are also reluctant or unable to provide care at these times (Statham and Mooney, 2003: forthcoming). Woodland et al (2002) also found that parents believed that group provision for children less than three years of age was inadequate, as was out of school care for older children. On the other hand, overall use of formal childcare has increased by 2% between 1999 and 2001 (Woodland et al, 2002, p 99). Among three-year-olds, attendance in formal childcare has risen from 19% in 1997 to 21% in 2000, and among four-year-olds this has risen from 11% to 15% between 1997 and 2000 (Blake et al, 2001). Use of Early Years education among three- and four-year-olds has also increased over the same period (Blake et al, 2001). In addition, 72% of parents have said that they would choose formal childcare as their ideal arrangement (Woodland et al, 2002, p 99).

Even so, many parents, including lone mothers, still rely on informal care provided by family and friends (NCOPF, 2002; Woodland et al, 2002). The government also recognises that informal care plays a major role in plugging the gaps in formal childcare (Strategy Unit, 2002, p 25). It is possible that informal care (as well as being cheaper than formal care) is preferred by many because it offers greater flexibility and allows easier management of the interface between childcare and workplace settings. Indeed, La Valle et al (2000) found that parents preferred flexible care provided by family and friends, followed by out of school clubs, childminders and nannies and that the odds of formal care reduced as the numbers of children in the family increased. Other evidence also shows that the propensity of mothers to be in employment decreases when there are more pre-school or school age children in the family, and even if mothers do work they are more likely to work part time (Paull and Taylor, 2002, p 27). This points to the possible complexity in coordinating childcare services when there is more than one child in the family, which has been shown to be problematic for parents (Bryson et al, 1999). However, flexible services are not the only concern; parents are also worried about the practicalities of getting children to and from care (Childcare Commission Report, 2001). There remains a gap in the research that explores how parents manage to coordinate childcare and educational needs for all the children in the family, how flexible work arrangements might affect this and how these relate to decisions about paid work.

The questions this study seeks to explore are therefore:

- How do working parents' coordinate childcare/educational needs for all their children?
- How do parents dovetail childcare and education with each other and with their working hours?
- How does this coordination function affect mothers' choices over employment and working hours?

These are important questions, not least because the current Labour government is keen to improve childcare services both as a means to increasing productivity in the UK in the global marketplace and to tackling child poverty. This commitment was renewed in the 2002 Spending Review. A further £1.5 billion was dedicated to expanding childcare services across England by 2005-06 and a new inter-departmental Childcare Unit was established to ensure that government policy in this area is joined-up (HM Treasury, 2002; Strategy Unit, 2002).

Policy context: reconciling work and family life

The Labour government is promoting the idea that families can and should be able to 'balance' their working and family lives (Home Office, 1998; DfEE, 2000). Numerous strategies have been put in place to help meet that objective, including improved rights to maternity, parental and paternal leave (not covered here). Other strategies are the Work–Life Balance Campaign, which aims to encourage employers to introduce flexible working practices and the National Childcare Strategy.

Under the Work–Life Balance Campaign, launched in 2000, employers are being encouraged (but not directed) to voluntarily introduce flexible work arrangements and to develop models of good practice. As described previously, this increasing flexibility in working hours is viewed positively by parents. However,

as Perrons (1998) points out, parental preferences for flexible work are often made in the context of inadequate or costly childcare provision. The government is, however, attempting to remedy these problems through the National Childcare Strategy.

The National Childcare Strategy in England was launched in 1998 and marked a sea change in the nature of childcare provision. It aims to improve the availability, affordability and quality of childcare in order to increase prosperity through employment, particularly for low-income and lone-parent families (DfEE, 1998). Many improvements have been made, including: an increase in the financial support for childcare costs for low-income families in receipt of Working Families' Tax Credit; new childcare places have been created for half a million children in England; and by March 2004 the target is to create a million more places (DfEE, 2001). There is also a guarantee of part-time places in early education for all three-year-olds by 2004 and the government has already succeeded in guaranteeing part-time early education for all four-year-olds where the parents want it (Strategy Unit, 2002). The childcare industry is being encouraged to provide extended opening hours and out of normal hours services through various funding packages. Moreover, building on the Sure Start initiative, more integrated childcare, educational and family support services are to be provided at the local level through Children's Centres (Strategy Unit, 2002). These are mainly targeted at the most deprived areas and form part of the government's broad strategy to deal with social exclusion by increasing the labour participation rates of lone parents to 70% and to halve child poverty by 2010 (Bertram and Pascal, 2001; DfEE, 2001; Strategy Unit, 2002). Indeed, spending allocated to childcare initiatives in England between 2001-04 stands at £8.2 billion, the bulk of which (£5.9 billion) is dedicated to free Early Years education for three- and four-year-old children (Strategy Unit, 2002, p 10).

Analysis of administrative records in England in 2001 (Skinner, 2002) confirms that there is an overall rise in the number of places in private nursery day care, in out of school clubs and holiday schemes, with the latter showing a threefold increase since 1997. There has also been a threefold increase in the numbers of children attending pre-school education in the private/voluntary sector between 1997 and 2001, although in the statutory pre-school education sector, the numbers of children attending has remained fairly static. However, alongside this, there has been a slight but consistent decrease in childminder and playgroup places. The decline in the numbers of childminders is particularly important as this potentially offers the greatest form of flexible care for parents of both pre-school and school age children and is one of the preferred types of care after informal care (La Valle et al, 2000). In particular, childminders are more likely than other private providers (day care nurseries, out of school clubs and playgroups) to offer care outside normal hours and at times that may vary frequently (Statham and Mooney, 2003: forthcoming). However, the decline in childminders is being tackled through the provision of start-up grants, improved recruitment and training packages, and by facilitating the development of childcare networks within the new Children's Centres and in the proposed expansion of extended childcare services offered within school premises (Strategy Unit, 2002).

Important as these developments are, many parents continue to face fragmented services in different institutional settings that operate different opening times (Penn, 2000; Randall, 2000). In particular, services across day care and early education are split and compartmentalised (Moss, 2001). The 2002 Spending Review, however, shows that the government remains committed to improvements, including providing greater integration of services. For example, the new inter-departmental Childcare Unit will be responsible for ensuring that 250,000 more childcare places are provided by 2006, although most of this increase will be through the establishment of Children's Centres in deprived areas (HM Treasury, 2002; Strategy Unit, 2002). The unit will also consider ways to encourage the integration of childcare and education services within schools themselves. Against this policy climate, the changes in flexible work practices and the complexity of childcare provision, it is important to understand more about the practicalities facing parents in coordinating childcare, education and employment arrangements in order to reconcile work and family life.

Methods

This report is based on a secondary analysis of qualitative data that was collected as part of a European study[3]. The study explored how parents in five countries reconciled work and family life and the author conducted the English component in 1999. Qualitative data was collected from semi-structured interviews with 40 mothers living in two separate areas within a middle-sized city in England. There were two selection criteria: respondents had to live in one of the areas and have at least one child under five years of age.

Choosing respondents

The city in England was chosen by the managers of the European project to correspond with the other four participating cities situated in mainland Europe. The two areas were chosen because they offered the potential to provide respondents with a range of different socioeconomic circumstances, but at the same time would help control for differences in access to local childcare provision. Area A predominately contained private housing, while Area B was predominately social housing. Potential respondents were contacted by letter via nurseries in primary schools, local playgroups and childminders situated within the two areas. This first strategy yielded 20 respondents from Area A, but only 11 from Area B. A second snowballing strategy was adopted targeting Area B, and a further 11 respondents agreed to take part, nine of which were interviewed. These respondents were likely to be using some kind of formal care (including pre-school education) and were therefore untypical, because other surveys show the majority of parents use informal care. In relation to socioeconomic characteristics of the areas, an analysis of child poverty rates of the two electoral wards within which the areas were situated confirms differences between them.

Table 1.1 shows that Area A was situated in a ward with a child poverty rate of 30.6%, which meant just under a third of children were living in families in receipt of Income Support or

---

[3] More details on the European study are presented in Appendix B.

Table 1.1: Child poverty rate in the two wards from which respondents were chosen

	Child poverty rate (%)[a]	Rank up from the most impoverished wards in England, Wales and Scotland in 1999[b]	% of wards with lower child poverty rate in England, Wales and Scotland in 1999
Area A	30.6	4,393	60
Area B	47.2	1,826	83
Lowest ranked ward in the city	54.1	1,108	90

Notes: [a] Child poverty rate is calculated as the number of children living in families receiving Income Support or Income Support-based Jobseeker's Allowance or Family Credit as a percentage of all children in 1999.
[b] N = 11,090; most impoverished = 1, least impoverished = 11,090.
Source: DETR (2000)

Income Support-based Jobseeker's Allowance or Family Credit. Ranking the ward on a deprivation index of child poverty with all wards in England, Wales and Scotland shows that Area A was ranked within the middle quintile range, with 60% of other wards having lower rates of child poverty. As might be expected, Area B was situated within a ward with a much higher rate of child poverty at 47.2%, but was still not the worst ward in the city (which had a rate of 54.1%). Area B was also ranked on the deprivation index in the top quintile range, with 83% of other wards having a lower rate of child poverty. Thus, Area A had an average rate of child poverty, while Area B fell into the top 20% of wards with the highest rates of child poverty. The characteristics of respondents to the current study demonstrates a range of different socioeconomic circumstances. These are described in Tables 1.2 and 1.3.

Respondent characteristics

The respondent characteristics show that the 40 parents were living in a mix of married (30), cohabiting (4) or lone-parent families (6), with married families making up the majority. Most families had two children, but a relatively high number (15) had three or four children. The average ages of children were young, aged five to seven depending on family type, but their ages ranged from one to eighteen years. A considerable number (16) had only pre-school children in the family (aged four or less) and the rest (24) had a mix of pre-school and older children. In eight families, there was at least one child from a parent's previous relationship living in the household. Most of the families also had at least one employed earner (35) and the most

common employment pattern was where the father worked full-time and the mother worked part time (20 families). Most of the mothers were in paid work (28), but most worked part time (21). However, only two of the six lone mothers were in paid work. The occupational status of employed fathers shows that approximately half were in professional and half in semi-skilled occupations. Employed mothers were predominately in unskilled work (11) or semi-skilled work (8), with about one third (9) in professional/managerial occupations.

Overall, the respondents demonstrate a broad range of circumstances in terms of marital, occupational and employment status and family characteristics. Although not a representative sample, the pattern of employment broadly reflects the national picture where the majority of mothers with dependent children work part time, there is a lower rate of employment among lone mothers and those using formal childcare tend to be in higher status occupations.

As described at the start of this chapter, access to suitable childcare is an important factor in mothers' employment and it is therefore important to set the scene of available services in the areas within which the families lived.

Local childcare provision

The parents in the two areas used three main primary schools. However, only two of these provided school nursery education for three- to four-year-olds. All the respondents who used school nursery education exclusively used that provided by both these schools.

Table 1.2: Respondent characteristics

	Married couples[a], N = 30	Cohabiting couples[a], N = 4	Lone parents, N = 6	Total
Number of children in the family				
1	4	–	–	4
2	16	2	3	21
3	7	1	1	9
4	3	1	2	6
Number of families with all children aged four or less	13	1	2	16
Number of families with children of mixed ages; over and under four years old	17	3	4	24
Average age of children	5	6	7	–
Number of families which include children from a previous relationship	4	2	2	8
Parental employment				
Both parents work/study full time[b]	5	1	n/a	6
One parent only works full time	6	1	1	8
One parent works full time, the other part time	19	1	n/a	20
One parent only works part time	–	–	1	1
All parents inactive/unemployed	–	1	4	5
Mothers' employment				
Mother works/studies full time	5	1	1	7
Mother works part time	19	1	1	21
Mother not in paid work	6	2	4	12

Notes: [a] Currently married or cohabiting and living with current partner.
[b] In three cases mothers were studying full time, and in one of those the father was also studying full time; one mother was paid a salary while studying to be a nurse.

Table 1.3: Respondent occupations

Occupations	Married couples		Cohabiting couples		Lone parents	Total
	Fathers	Mothers	Fathers	Mothers	Mothers	
Managerial/Professional occupations[a]	14	8	1	1	–	24
Skilled/Semi-skilled[b]	14	6	1	–	2	23
Unskilled[c]	2	10	1	1	–	14
Total	30	24	3	2	2	

Notes: [a] Includes: administrators/managers, accountants, IT consultants, engineers, doctors, registered nurses, social workers, journalists, teachers.
[b] Includes: bank officers, electricians, mechanics, VDU operators, painters and decorators, lorry drivers, students, cooks, caterers, self-employed merchandisers, welders, fitters and prison support workers.
[c] Includes: administration assistants, nurse assistants, receptionists, retail, catering and call centre workers, labourers, bar workers and window cleaners.

Table 1.4: Number of registered childcare providers in the two electoral wards within which respondents lived[a]

	Child-minders	Private day nurseries	Out of school clubs
Area A	13	2	2
Area B	7	0	0
Total for the city	279	30	20

Note: [a] The city had 29 electoral wards in total.
Source: Local Authority Childcare Audit (1999)

The number of registered childcare providers in the two areas is described in Table 1.4. This shows that Area B, located within the ward with the higher child poverty rate, was not as well serviced as Area A, with the lower child poverty rate. The two out of school clubs and the two private nurseries were all located within the ward in which Area A was situated. Area A also contained almost double the number of registered childminders.

The data demonstrates that respondents who lived in Area B could also use the out of school clubs situated in Area A, as the clubs collected children from the three primary schools that the respondents used. Similarly, as the actual geographical location of the private nurseries was fairly central to both areas (even though they were situated within Area A's ward boundary), they were accessible to respondents from both areas. However, up to five other private nurseries outside the areas were also used, including three based near to the place of employment or study. It is harder to be sure about 'real' access to childminders, as the study did not record whether all the childminders used were officially registered or not (for example, some of the parents used 'nannies' who provided care in the family home). This demonstrates the difficulties of using aggregated ward level data to describe the 'real' level of access to childcare that a given group of people might have. Nevertheless, it gives an indication of the services available and shows there was a fairly broad range of provision situated locally.

Data collection

The data collection methods involved semi-structured face-to-face interviews using a topic guide. The topic guide was originally set by the European team to ensure consistency in data collection across the countries, but in discussion was adapted by the author to reflect the particular childcare services in the UK (see Appendix B). The interviews lasted between one and two hours and all were tape recorded and transcribed in full. Interviews were conducted following written consent from respondents and further verbal consent was sought immediately prior to the interview in regard to data storage and secondary analysis, whereby the tapes (stored in a university in Denmark) would be accessible to other researchers with the permission of the European team.

Data analysis

A computer package (Atlas ti) was used to store, code and retrieve the data from the transcriptions. Themes were identified through an inductive and deductive approach and charts were constructed manually to identify similarities and differences across respondents. In order to explore the relative ease or difficulty in coordinating childcare and work commitments, the sample was grouped according to the mothers' employment status: a full-time working group, a part-time working group and a non-working group. These groupings represented a continuum of employment participation.

The experiences of each group are reported separately in the following three chapters. Before that, however, a key concept that emerged from the data – 'coordination points' – which helps to cast light on the practicalities of reconciling childcare and work commitments, is presented in the next chapter.

2

Coordinating childcare

The ways in which parents coordinate the childcare and educational needs of children alongside work commitments are often ignored. The routines and strategies they set up tend to be taken for granted and are viewed as a private responsibility. This chapter aims to elevate these taken for granted elements by presenting some case studies which show exactly what is involved for parents in getting themselves to and from work and in taking children to and from care and education. It then presents the concept of 'coordination points' that has arisen out of the data. This concept refers to the interface between different care/educational settings that have to be managed by parents repeatedly at critical times of the day. It helps expose the management strategies parents use to coordinate work and caring.

Examples of coordination

It can be seen in the case study in Figures 2.1 and 2.2 that for this simple real-life example (where there are two children in the family and both parents work full time) there are a number of daily journeys made by each individual in the family going to and from work, childcare and education. In total, 15 individual journeys occur daily. The mother does six journeys, which revolve around taking both children to and from home, childcare and education (although the grandfather helps out sometimes) and getting herself to and from work. The youngest child does four journeys; in the morning from home to school to private nursery (two), and in the evening from private nursery to the childminder's house and then to home (two). The oldest child does three journeys; from home to school in the morning, from school to the childminder's house in the afternoon and from the childminder's

house to home in the evening. The children share only two journeys together per day. The father does two journeys, to and from work (although he does leave work early on a Friday and collects the youngest from private nursery). In this case study, the mother's preferred mode of transport was a bike. Other mothers in this study also used bikes and others used cars to cover similar journeys; none used public transport.

It is important to consider these journeys as existing separately from one another, even though some are connected. First, because they are real events and reflect the reality of some families lives; second, because each journey is punctuated by different time deadlines (the start and finish times for nursery, school and work differ); lastly, because if there were fewer children in the family the number of journeys would be reduced. Paradoxically, considering the children's journeys as separate events exposes their interconnectivity. For example, a delay in one would have knock-on effects for the rest, with potentially serious consequences for the mother's employment record if she is delayed in the morning and consequences for care of the children if she is delayed in picking them up in the evening. In effect, this mother has to manage six critical deadlines in a day; two for each of the children's childcare and two for her employment (starting and finishing work on time). Simultaneously, however, she also has to manage three changes in care settings across the day, from home to childcare/education in the *morning*, from school to after school care in the *afternoon*, and from childcare to home in the *evening*. They represent the coordination points in the day (see Figure 2.3) and these have to be managed to provide a seamless package of care for her children.

Figure 2.1: Example of daily journeys a family makes in relation to home, childcare/education and work

---

The family

This example refers to one of the seven families in which both parents work full time. This family has one of the simplest sets of arrangements for childcare. There are two children; one is six years old and the other is 13 months old. They use a private nursery all day for the youngest child, and a mix of school and after school care provided by a childminder for the oldest child. The mother takes the major responsibility for transporting the children to and from the home to school/childcare, although the grandfather also helps one or two days of the week and the father one day a week. The distance from the family home to the father's workplace is 45 minutes by car and the mother's workplace is 10 minutes away by bicycle.

Actual journeys in the day

Mornings
The mother leaves home with both children and takes the oldest to school first and then takes the youngest to private nursery and then travels to work by bicycle (total three journeys).

After school
The childminder collects the oldest child from school and then takes him to her home and cares for him until the parents finish work.

Evenings
The mother travels from work by bicycle to collect the youngest child from private nursery, then travels to the childminder's home to pick up the oldest child and then takes both children home (three journeys).

Actual number of individual daily journeys by family members

Mother = 6[a]   Oldest child = 3
Father = 2[a] (to and from work)   Youngest child = 4
Total journeys for the family = 15

Note: [a] The grandfather helps out by taking the oldest child to school some days and the father collects the youngest child on a Friday from the private nursery.

Figure 2.2: The daily journeys made by a family to and from home, school, private nursery and the workplace

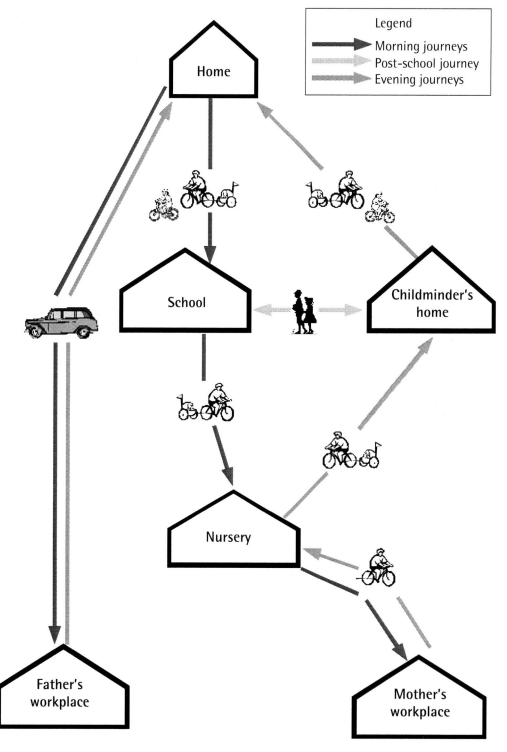

Father collects child from nursery one day per week

Figure 2.3: Daily coordination points

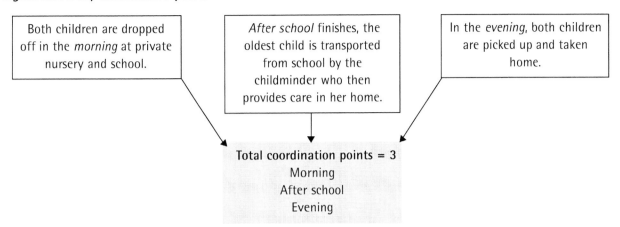

| Both children are dropped off in the *morning* at private nursery and school. | *After school* finishes, the oldest child is transported from school by the childminder who then provides care in her home. | In the *evening,* both children are picked up and taken home. |

Total coordination points = 3
Morning
After school
Evening

Coordination points

Coordination points represent those times in the day when children need to be taken to and from different childcare/educational settings. For parents using full-time childcare outside the home there are at least two daily points; dropping children off in the morning and picking them up in the evening. Potentially, however, the greater the number of providers used then the more coordination points in a day. The previous case study is one of the simplest set of arrangements with just three coordination points; other families in the study had five to manage. However, it is important to make a distinction between coordination points and the number of journeys an individual child or parent may make in a day. Even if parents do not actually transport children themselves, they still have to arrange these journeys and make sure that different childcare settings are dovetailed together with the minimum of difficulty for the children.

It is reasonable to assume, therefore, that the key to successful management is that work and care settings are in close proximity to one another, or that there is access to a fast and convenient mode of transport, and/or that parents can rely on someone else to transport children across care settings (including to and from the home), and/ or that parents have flexible work arrangements. Clearly, this management task has both a spatial dimension in which the proximity of work, care settings and the home have to be negotiated both temporally and physically, and a time dimension in which events must happen at predetermined hours of the day. Moreover, the successful operation of this management task requires time and effort in its own right and perhaps a considerable degree of skill.

Certainly, some forms of childcare provision take account of these spatial and time dimensions. In this study for example, after school clubs (AFSCs), while providing wrap-around care[1], were also situated within close proximity to primary schools, if not within the schools. They provided walkers to collect children at school finishing times and transport them to the club, providing a seamless service. However, in this study this management service was only available to primary school aged children. Most importantly, no similar management service existed within school nurseries or private nurseries to take pre-school age children to and from these different providers, thus the service was interrupted across these different providers. Alternatively, childminders/nannies and informal carers could help in transporting children in these circumstances to bridge the gap. This is clearly demonstrated in the model in Figure 2.4.

While working parents may not face problems managing the *post-school* coordination point for their primary school aged children (as management and wrap-around care was all provided as part of the AFSC service), this was not always the case for pre-school aged children. Thus it is helpful to make a distinction between the *management task* of ensuring children are transported between different providers at key coordination points in the day and the provision of *wrap-around care*. For example, it should not be assumed that all forms of wrap-around care (which can be provided by any of the formal or informal providers) also automatically offer support with transporting children across different providers. Similarly, it cannot be

---

[1] Wrap-around care is that provided to wrap around the working and school day.

Figure 2.4: Model of the management task in relation to coordination points and wrap-around care

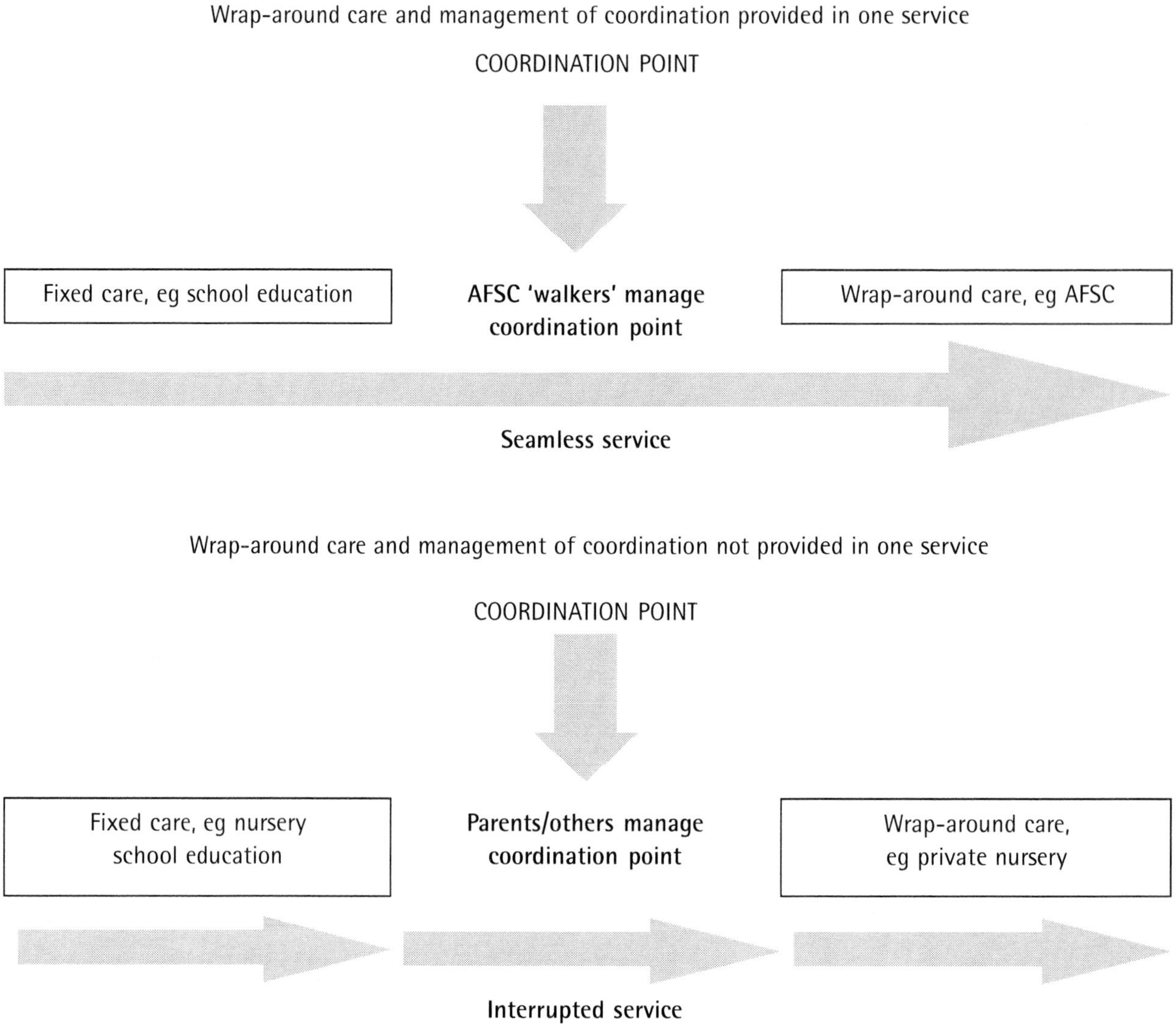

Wrap-around care and management of coordination provided in one service

COORDINATION POINT

Fixed care, eg school education	AFSC 'walkers' manage coordination point	Wrap-around care, eg AFSC

Seamless service

Wrap-around care and management of coordination not provided in one service

COORDINATION POINT

Fixed care, eg nursery school education	Parents/others manage coordination point	Wrap-around care, eg private nursery

Interrupted service

assumed that where someone provides support to transport children across providers, they also provide wrap-around care. Gaps in provision can therefore exist both at coordination points and in wrap-around care.

Summary

In order to appreciate the full complexity of managing childcare and work commitments, it is necessary to consider the management of coordination points separately but alongside the types of care used. It is also important to consider the question of whether the number of mothers' working hours and the times of day in which they take place make it easier or harder to coordinate work and care. Certainly, flexible, part-time and non-standard hours of employment are seen to be facilitators of mothers'

employment. Normative beliefs would also predict that full-time work for mothers would be the most difficult to coordinate and manage, that part-time work would be the easiest and that non-working mothers would have little or no coordination problems to worry about. Indeed, research evidence shows that the majority of mothers working part time do not want full-time jobs, that where mothers go on to have more than one child their hours of employment reduce and that some of the main barriers to mothers' employment relate to the availability, suitability, cost and quality of childcare and to inflexible work practices. In order to test these normative beliefs and to consider the impact of the nature of maternal employment on coordination, the rest of the report examines coordination points for three groups independently; full-time working mothers, part-time working mothers and non-working mothers.

3

Coordinating childcare and full-time paid work

This chapter describes the work and childcare arrangements of the full-time working mothers, and then considers the strategies used to manage coordination points. First, it shows the family characteristics of this group of full-time working mothers.

Family characteristics

There were seven families where the mothers worked full time when the interview was conducted (full-time work was defined as 31 hours per week or more). Two lived in the poorer Area B. Five were married couples and there was one cohabiting couple and one lone-parent family, although in one of the married

families there were children in the family from the mother's past relationship. The children were aged six on average, but the oldest child was aged 14. Most families had one or two children (five). All the families had only one child of pre-school age (aged four or less). Overall, family size was relatively small (compared to part-time and non-working families, which are discussed in Chapters Four and Five).

Childcare and work arrangements

Table 3.2 describes the mothers' working hours and the childcare services used. Four mothers worked full time and two mothers studied full time; all worked regular office type hours. The remaining mother worked shifts, which also covered weekends and nights. The total hours of work varied between 35 and 40 hours a week. The mothers' occupations included bank officer, administrators and a student nurse; and the fathers' occupations included retailer, self-employed caterer, managers, engineer and student. Given that only two full-time working mothers lived in the poorer Area B, it is difficult to make any meaningful comparison on the basis of socioeconomic status. Interestingly, however, the one lone parent who worked full-time did not live in the poorer area. Nevertheless, it is relatively simple to map and understand the working hours of these mothers, but this is not the case when considering their childcare arrangements.

All seven respondents used formal care for their pre-school aged children: this included private fee-paying nurseries (six cases) or a nanny (one case). This care was often combined with free school nursery or grandparent care (four cases).

Table 3.1: Family characteristics of full-time working mothers

	Number of families
Marital status	
Married	5
Cohabiting	1
Lone parent	1
Number of children in the family	
1	2
2	3
3	1
4	1
Number of children in the family aged four or less	
1	7
Number of families which include children from a previous relationship	1
Average age of children (range)	6 (1-14)
Total number of families	7

Table 3.2 : Weekly childcare arrangements and mothers' working hours, full-time working/studying mothers

Case number[a]	Mothers' total work hours	Mothers' type of work hours	Latest time mother finishes work	Ages of all children in the family[b]	Age of pre-school child	Hours of childcare for pre-school children (expressed in hours and minutes)					Total school hours	Weekly hours after school care for school-age children[c]	Total weekly hours childcare all children
						Private nursery	Childminder	Nanny	Grand-parent	School nursery			
A-02	35	Day	5pm	10, 4	4	28.45	–	–	–	14.35	43.20	12.30[e]	55.50[e]
A-03	37	Day	6pm	6, 2	2	47.30[d]	–	–	–	n/a	47.30	11.15	58.45
A-05	35	Day	4pm	3	3	–	–	22.55	–	12.30	35.25	n/a	35.25
A-25	30+ varies	Day	4pm	13, 9, 7, 4	4	14	–	–	–	14.35	28.35	10	38.35
A-38	37	Day	5.15pm	6, 1	1	44.35	–	–	–	n/a	44.35	11.15	55.50
B-29	35	Shifts (+ nightshift)	varies	2	2	20	–	–	4-14[e]	n/a	24[e]	n/a	24[e]
B-33	35[e]	Day	5 pm	14, 9, 3	3	35	–	–	–	–	35	varies	35[e]

Notes: [a] A = more affluent Area A; B = less affluent Area B.

[b] Youngest child in all cases pre-school age (< 5).

[c] Where more than one school age child, they tended to go to the same AFSC at the same time, the hours counted therefore refer to the time in AFSC and are not multiplied by the numbers of children in the family attending.

[d] Two different nurseries used on a weekly basis.

[e] Hours of childcare varies and amount is therefore approximate; likely to use more hours than this.

Additionally, all five parents who had school age children also used after school care, either in the form of an after school club (AFSC) or a childminder. Thus, none relied on just one form of childcare. This presents quite a complex picture of childcare among a mere seven respondents. The interesting question is how did the parents manage the coordination points; that is, transporting children across different care settings?

Coordination points

For this sample of seven mothers working or studying full-time, five coordination points in the day were identified, as follows and in Figure 3.1:

1. Morning, 8-9am
2. Lunchtime, 11.30am-1pm
3. Post-school, 3-3.30pm
4. Early evening, 4-6pm
5. Late evening, 9-10pm

Figure 3.1: Model of coordination points for full-time working/studying mothers in a typical working week

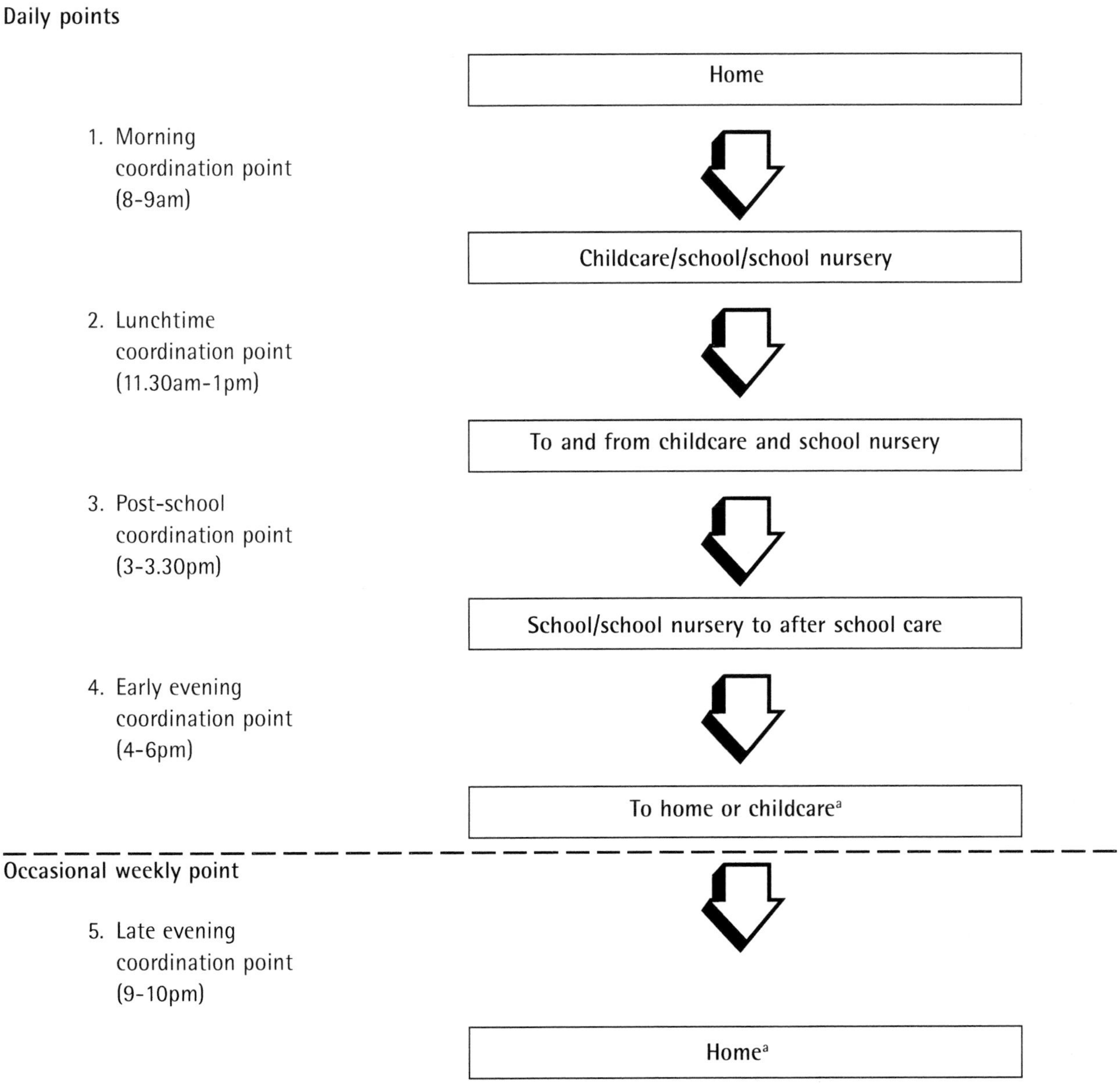

Daily points

1. Morning coordination point (8-9am)

2. Lunchtime coordination point (11.30am-1pm)

3. Post-school coordination point (3-3.30pm)

4. Early evening coordination point (4-6pm)

Occasional weekly point

5. Late evening coordination point (9-10pm)

Home

Childcare/school/school nursery

To and from childcare and school nursery

School/school nursery to after school care

To home or childcare[a]

Home[a]

Note: [a] One child went to the grandmother for care until the mother finished working late in the evening, or she went to the grandmother to stay overnight when the mother worked a night shift.

Table 3.3: Number of daily coordination points managed by individual families

Two coordination points daily	Three coordination points daily	Four coordination points daily
1	4	2

The late evening coordination point was only relevant to one respondent who worked shifts and therefore it did not occur on a daily but on a weekly basis.

Most parents (four) had to manage three points daily. Two of the parents had to mange four points daily and one parent had to manage only two points (see Table 3.3). Various strategies were identified that enabled parents to manage these points in the day.

Management strategies

The parents used a mixture of strategies to manage coordination points. Importantly, the particular combination of strategies increased in complexity depending on the number of people involved, the number and ages of children in the family, the number of different childcare providers used, parents' working hours and the degree of flexibility over working hours. The strategies identified included:

- arranging regular informal support with coordination points;
- arranging regular formal support with coordination points;
- arranging insurance back-up support.

Arranging regular informal and/or formal support with coordination points

Arranging support with coordination points starts from the premise that mothers took the major responsibility for management and that they sought support from others, including fathers. Evidence shows that mothers do take the major responsibility for management of childcare (Dex, 1999; Woodland et al, 2002). Certainly, the picture presented by mothers in this study was that fathers were in a supporting role. The fathers may have had a different perspective, but only two were interviewed. It is therefore difficult to be certain about the fathers' level of involvement with management per se although,

as will be shown, many were involved in transporting children at coordination points.

All seven full-time working mothers relied on informal support for at least one coordination point in the day, even though they also regularly transported children themselves. Six mothers also relied on formal support for at least one coordination point (see Table 3.4). Informal support refers to that provided by fathers, other family members, friends and neighbours, whereas, formal support is provided by paid child carers, commonly AFSCs, childminders and nannies. To give a picture of what is involved on a daily basis, each of the five coordination points is described separately.

The *morning coordination point* refers to the interface between home and childcare and school. The greatest amount of support was received at this time; four fathers helped regularly by transporting at least one child in the family to formal care/school, as did two friends/ neighbours and two grandparents. The main reasons for needing this support included mothers starting work before formal childcare began (as was the case for the two mothers who had only one child, cases A-05 and B-29) or mothers not being able to manage multiple journeys with children and arrive at work on time. No one received formal support in the morning.

The *lunchtime coordination point* mainly occurred as a result of pre-school aged children (aged between three and four years) attending *both* part-time school nursery and other care on a daily basis: the crossover point occurring at lunchtime. This was the case for three families. One other mother (case B-29) had a coordination point occurring at lunchtime even though her child was too young for pre-school education; this was mainly related to her shift patterns. The kinds of support used at lunchtime varied. One mother (a lone parent) relied on a mixture of support from a neighbour or grandmother, or informal support from the private nursery manager (the nursery manager helped on the basis of goodwill and did not charge for the

Table 3.4: Persons providing informal and [formal] support with daily coordination points in a typical working week

Case number	Ages of children	Time mother finishes work	Daily coordination points					Total people per week including parents	
			Morning 8–9am	Lunchtime 11.30am–1pm	Post-school 3–3.30pm	Early evening 4–6pm	Late evening 9–10pm	Informal	Formal
A-02[a]	10, 4	5pm	Neighbour A	Grandparent Neighbour B PN manager[b] Mother	[AFSC]	Mother	n/a	5	1
A-03	6, 2	6pm	Mother Father	n/a	[AFSC]	Mother Father Neighbour	n/a	3	1
A-05	3	4pm	Father	[Nanny]	n/a	Mother	n/a	2	1
A-25	13, 9, 7, 4	4pm	Mother Friend	Mother Father Friend	[AFSC]	Mother	n/a	3	1
A-38	6, 1	5.15pm	Mother Grandfather	n/a	Grandmother [Childminder]	Mother Father	n/a	4	1
B-29	2	Varies (shifts)	Mother Father Grandparent	Mother Grandparent	n/a	Mother	Mother	3	–
B-33	14, 9, 3	5pm	Mother Father	n/a	[AFSC]	Mother Father	n/a	2	1
Total (not mothers)			8	7	6	4	0	22 (including mothers)	6

Notes: [a] = Lone-parent family; [b] PN manager = private nursery manager.
A = more affluent Area A; B = less affluent Area B.

service). As the mother said, "I rely on anyone I can get to do it". If all else failed, she could leave work and transport the child herself. Therefore, up to four people in a week could be involved with this one child at lunchtime. Another mother, a student nurse, relied on the grandmother if she could not collect the child herself at lunchtime. A third mother was a full-time student and, depending on her schedule, she could leave college and do the transporting herself, but frequently she had to rely on her husband to leave work and do it, or rely on friends if he could not. Only one mother relied on formal support from the nanny every day at the lunchtime point.

The *post-school coordination point* refers to the interface between school and after school care and most of the support at this point was formal. An AFSC was used in four cases and a childminder in one case. The childminder was specifically employed to collect the family's older child from school and provide wrap-around care until the parents finished work, although a grandmother also provided informal support in the same way on one day of the week. The two other cases did not have children of school age. Thus, all those with school age children used formal support and one also used informal support.

The *early evening coordination point* refers to the time when children are collected from care and taken home after parents have finished work. All seven mothers managed to pick up their children at this point most days of the week, but not always. One mother relied on a mixture of support from the father and a neighbour to collect the children some evenings, another relied on the father to help one day a week, while in the third case the father and mother did it together. No one used formal support at this time of day.

The *late evening coordination point* referred only to the student nurse who had to collect her child from the grandmother's house when she worked an evening or night shift.

Overall, among these seven families, in a typical working week a total of 28 people could be involved in transporting children to and from different care settings, including mothers, fathers, grandparents, friends/neighbours, AFSCs, childminders and nannies. Private nursery staff

were not involved in transporting children, apart from the one incidence of a private nursery manager doing this as a favour without payment[1]. The greatest amount of *informal* support was received at the morning and lunchtime coordination points, while the greatest amount of *formal* support was received at the post-school point. The lunchtime coordination point occurred mainly (but not exclusively) as a result of school nursery education times and, as will be shown in the case study, this was one of the most difficult points to deal with.

Interestingly, the lone parent with two children received the greatest amount of support from others (five people). Whereas, one might have expected that families with three children (case B-33) or four children (case A-25) would have had the greatest support, but in both of these cases the fathers could be involved at least twice per day, an option not available to the lone parent. Even so, for all the respondents, while informal and formal support was arranged to cover routine childcare needs, it did not cover less routine or exceptional needs. For that, parents had to arrange back-up care with coordination points.

Arranging insurance back-up support

Arranging back-up support with coordination points as an insurance when the routine might change was often an implicit activity and therefore it was not easy to get an accurate picture for all the respondents. Strategies that were obvious, however, included relying on family or friends/neighbours to step in at the last minute to transport children across providers and sometimes to also provide wrap-around care. These people could be in addition to those providing regular informal support with coordination points. As a last resort, mothers (rarely fathers) would also rely on the goodwill of their employer to give them a short period off work to transport the children themselves.

---

[1] It seemed that this was only possible because the school nursery and private nursery were very close to one another (a 10-minute walk).

The kind of situations in which this back-up support was needed was where the parents' (usually the mothers') work schedule altered, where the children's schedule altered, or where the main carer (usually a childminder or nanny) was sick. In the latter situation wrap-around care was usually also required. A key feature of managing back-up support for coordination points was the insurance element, in which the mothers would build and nurture reciprocal relationships with friends/neighbours to provide support 'just in case'. There was evidence that where these mothers could not act as an insurance back-up in return (as they were working full time), they would provide childcare support for friends/neighbours at the weekends or holidays.

The reciprocal expectation attached to these friendships proved easy to manage and a bonus for some, but difficult for others. For example, in the case where the nanny was shared with friends, the mother said this was a bonus as there were four parents to call on in emergencies. Here was a readymade informal network closely tied into formal nanny care that was nurtured on a daily basis as an insurance with managing coordination points. This was distinguished from needing emergency care when the nanny was sick; in that situation grandparents who lived two hundred miles away were called on to provide childcare.

In another case involving a full-time student, reciprocal relationships were difficult to manage. The difficulties occurred when she had to attend work placements outside the area as part of her course. During these times, she relied on a mix of friends/neighbours to provide wrap-around care prior to school and to manage the morning coordination point by taking her children to school and formal childcare. She found this hard to deal with, as it was impossible to provide the same level of support in return. Consequently, she did not only feel beholden to her friends/neighbours, but she was also worried that she was a burden on them and they might soon begin to avoid her. She tried to offer payment for this support but her friends had refused, perhaps because they did not want to make a commitment to offer this care. As an alternative, she tried to offer childcare in the school holidays in return, but in her eyes, this did not seem to rebalance the relationships sufficiently. This demonstrates the precarious nature of this form of insurance support and how it seems to

operate with a mental balance sheet requiring childcare time offered in return; time being a rare commodity for mothers working/studying full time. It was more difficult to see this kind of reciprocity operating with family back-up support.

Overall, this focus on coordination points among a mere seven full-time working/studying mothers exposes an often hidden, complex network of informal, formal and insurance type support that is managed alongside but is often *additional* to full-time formal childcare. In order to have a better picture of the factors that influence the degree of complexity in managing coordination points, two cases studies will be presented: one of the most complex scenarios and one of the simplest.

Complex management of daily coordination points

Case study one stands out as a masterpiece of parental organisation. These parents tended to be self-reliant in managing the coordination points, but this was only achievable because of the close proximity of both parents' workplaces to the home and to the sites of childcare/education and also because the mother could take advantage of flexitime hours. This self-reliance, however, was not without cost. First, the mother had to manage a balance sheet of debit and credit working hours. This demonstrates a double bind with flexitime hours; not only do flexi hours have to be paid back, but they involve time and effort in managing them. Second, both parents had to coordinate each other's work commitments on a daily basis to a finely tuned level. The mother said this period of their family life was one of the most stressful. Certainly, it is not hard to imagine how any small alteration in either of the parent's work schedule could have wreaked havoc on arrangements. However, these parents did have insurance back-up support. First, their employers were fairly understanding and flexible, partly as a result of a long employment history with the parents (the mother had worked for her employer for 20 years and the father for 25 years). Second, both parents had lived in the neighbourhood all their lives and thus both sets of grandparents lived close by and could be called upon in an emergency.

Case study one: Complex management of daily coordination points

This family had two children aged six and two at the time of the interview (case A-03). This most complex set of childcare arrangements did not relate to the time the study was conducted, but to what happened a few years previously when the oldest child was aged four and attending school nursery and the youngest child was a baby. The factors that contributed to the complexity were the part-time nature and the fixed hours of school nursery provision, the difficulties of dovetailing the times of school nursery care with the then equally inflexible hours of private nursery care, the difficulties of transporting the oldest child between the two types of provision, the rules surrounding the mothers' flexitime hours and the fact that the parents did not call on regular family support to manage coordination points. Their childcare arrangements will now be described around the various coordination points in the day.

At the *morning coordination point*, the parents shared dropping off the children. The father took the baby to full-time private nursery care at around 8am and the mother walked the older child to school nursery around 8.50am. Both provisions were within a very short distance from the family home (less than half a mile). The father would proceed to work by bike and the mother would go by car; both parents worked within less than two miles of the family home. Even so, the mother estimated that it took her 30 minutes to drop off the child at school nursery and travel to work. It took the father 10-15 minutes as he worked slightly closer to the family home and travelling by bike allowed him to avoid traffic congestion. This shared arrangement was suitable as the father had to begin work at 8.30am, while the mother could choose to start work after 9am because of employment flexitime practices.

At the *lunchtime coordination point*, arrangements were more complicated. The four-year-old finished school nursery at 11.45am and could not go to private nursery until the afternoon session officially began at 1pm. To care for him during that time, the father had to take an early lunch hour (between 11.30 and 12.30pm) to collect the child from school nursery at 11.45am. The father travelled to the nursery from work by bike. The mother would then return home by car during her lunch hour between 12.15 and 1.15pm to take over from the father (allowing him to return to work) and to take the child to private nursery for 1pm. Both children would then be cared for in the same private nursery until 5pm when one of the parents came to collect them. Overall, this absence of formal childcare for one hour and 15 minutes at the lunchtime coordination point involved two hours of parental care to fill the gap. (However, the following term the four-year-old changed from attending school nursery in the morning to attending in the afternoon. The same strategies of sharing the lunchtime coordination point between the parents was adopted, but they now had the added problem of no care for the oldest child post-school nursery (from 3 to 5pm) as he was too young to attend an AFSC and the private nursery would not take him back for a couple of hours of after school care. During that term they relied on a next-door neighbour (who they paid) to collect him from school nursery and provide wrap-around care until the parents finished work.)

The *early evening coordination point* was also shared by the parents. The mother collected the children most evenings after work and she relied on her car to get her there on time before the nursery closed. However, the father would pick up the children at least one night a week to allow the mother to work late (until 6pm) in order for her to make up the time lost in arriving late (after 9am) in the mornings. The flexitime rules were such that she could neither be 10 hours over or under the total number of hours she was expected to work in a month. She was also prohibited from working later than 6pm as this was into 'overtime hours' that she was not entitled to. This meant that she frequently see-sawed between debit and credit hours and she had to keep a constant balance sheet and make adjustments to meet her employment obligations.

Yet, successful as these parents were, they could not go it alone all the time. For one term, they had to rely on assistance from a neighbour to collect their youngest child from school nursery at the post-school coordination point and provide wrap-around care until the parents finished work in the evenings. This care was needed because the child was too young to attend an AFSC and the private nursery that he attended in the mornings would not provide after nursery school care. Here we see how the age of the child was more influential in creating coordination difficulties than the fact that there were two children in the family. These difficulties (related to age and to the use of part-time pre-school education in school nurseries) were not unique, but were faced by all three full-time working parents who used this form of care. Informal or formal support was needed to transport children at lunchtime or post-school, depending on whether school nursery was in the morning or afternoon. It seemed to be much simpler for those who used childminders or nannies as they managed the relevant coordination points on behalf of parents as part of their job – this is given further weight by the simpler case study.

Simple management of daily coordination points

As in case study one, the parents in case study two were also able to share the management of coordination points, but this was a result of working in a parental shift pattern[2]. This shift pattern was a deliberate choice made by the mother; she had changed jobs to fit around the working hours of the father (she started work early in the morning and he started work in the afternoon). Thus, the father transported the child in the morning to school nursery and the mother collected the child from care in the evening and took her home. This meant that the parents managed the morning and early evening coordination point by themselves, but they could not provide back-up support for each other at these coordination points (if the father had to go to work early one day, for example, it could cause problems). However, they did have back-up from the other parents who shared the nanny if such a situation occurred. They also had

---

[2] Parental shift pattern is where both parents worked opposite, or nearly opposite, hours to one another.

Case study two: Simple management of daily coordination points

This case study family had only one child aged three years old (case A-05). The factors that contributed to the simplicity of managing daily coordination points included: the use of a shared nanny (they shared a full-time nanny with friends); the close proximity of the care settings (that is, the homes of the families sharing the nanny); the close proximity of the families' homes to the nursery school; and the different employment hours of the parents.

At the *morning coordination point*, the father walked the child to school nursery every day at about 8.50am. This journey took 10-15 minutes. The mother was unable to manage this coordination point as her hours of employment were between 8am and 4pm Monday to Friday, whereas the father was available as he worked in the afternoon, evenings and at weekends as the normal requirement of his job.

At the *lunchtime coordination point*, the nanny collected the child from school nursery every day. The nanny would then provide wrap-around care until the mother finished work at 4pm. This nanny was shared with another family and the care took place in each of the families' homes on an alternating basis. Both homes were within 15 minutes walking distance from the school nursery and about five minutes walking distance from one another.

At the *early evening coordination point*, the mother would either pick up her child from the other family's house or go straight home from work when the nanny was providing care in the family home. The journey time from work to picking up her child by car was 5-10 minutes irrespective of whether the child was in their own home or the other family's home.

formal support from the nanny who managed the lunchtime coordination point attached to school nursery times and we can see from the first case study that this care simplified the management of the lunchtime coordination point and probably also reduced family stress. Importantly, while having only one child in this family made coordination simpler, this did not mean that if they went on to have a second child that coordination would necessarily become more complex. This was because the father would still have enough time in the morning to transport more than one child to care/education and the nanny potentially could have the flexibility to change her working hours to fit around the family's needs. Thus, it is the combination of flexible nanny care and the parental shift hours, rather than the number of children in the family that contributes to the simplicity of this family's coordination arrangements. However, if either of the parents' working hours changed, particularly the father's, then this might create considerable difficulties.

The evidence has presented some, but not all, of the management strategies that these full-time working parents used, as over time different ones had been adopted depending on circumstances. In addition, parents could have different strategies in place to manage care in the school holidays, but it was not possible to explore these in depth. However, they serve to demonstrate how additional strategies might have been needed at different times of the year. Nevertheless, taking the past and current management strategies together, these included:

Informal support:

- Relying on fathers:
  - Adopting a parental childcare shift pattern to maximise paternal support.
  - Fathers' adjusting working hours to help with transporting children (for example, leaving work early or taking shorter lunchtime breaks).
  - Fathers' giving up work and becoming the full-time child carer.
- Relying on regular family support (usually, but not always, grandparents).
- Relying on regular support from friends/ neighbours (paid in kind or in money).

Formal support:

- Relying on nannies, childminders and/or AFSCs.
- Relying on flexitime working hours.

Insurance back-up:

- Relying on non-reciprocal family support.
- Relying on reciprocal support from friends/ neighbours (paid in kind).
- Relying on the goodwill of employer and work colleagues to release parents from work for short periods of time.
- Booking and paying for formal childcare as a back-up that may never be used.
- Splitting the weekly childcare of a single child across similar providers (using two private nurseries instead of one, for example) because one offered more extended opening hours.

The management strategies attached to coordination points expose the gaps in care that can be created as a result of different institutional arrangements, particularly the gap created between private nursery and school nursery and the lack of an after (nursery) school service for pre-school aged children. This gap is closely related to the age of the child, where they have to be aged three to four years to use school nursery education. However, the gaps can also be seen to result from parental choice; for example, it was not necessary for parents to send their children to school nursery, they could have used private nursery care for the whole day and thereby have reduced the coordination complexity. More implicitly, their decision to work full time may also have had an impact. This element of parental choice is worth exploring further.

Parental choice

All the full-time working/studying mothers (bar one) used a private nursery for their pre-school aged children and they gave multiple reasons for choosing this form of care, including:

- Feeling that their child would experience greater social interaction than in other forms of care, such as a childminder (three cases).

- Having bad experiences with poor quality care provided by childminders in the past (two cases).
- Wanting their child to remain in one place during the day and not to be taken backwards and forwards with other children when the childminder collected them from school, and so on (two cases).
- Choosing the private nursery for its convenient location to workplace, study place and home (three cases), despite inconvenient opening hours (one case).
- Choosing the private nursery for quality of care, even though inconveniently located to work and home (one case).

They also used a school nursery because:

- Parents thought it provided educational and developmental input not available in the private nursery (three cases).
- It reduced the cost of childcare (two cases).

In considering these reasons, it seems that the private nursery was chosen on the basis of judgements about the quality and type of care offered in an institutional setting, even if in some cases it was also inconvenient (in terms of opening times or location). School nursery was chosen, however, because it offered something additional to private nursery care – education, and in some cases it also reduced the costs of care.

This helps to explain why the parents in the complex case study provided their own lunchtime care for their oldest child in the gap between school nursery and private nursery. They did this because they believed the school nursery offered additional educational input and because it helped cut the costs of formal childcare. Simultaneously, they chose private nursery care in the first instance, as opposed to a childminder/nanny, because they perceived this form of care as better for their children. However, in making the choice to send their child to both providers, they could not be relieved of the management of coordination points surrounding school nursery times as this was not provided as part of the private or school nursery service. In this case, however, the private nursery, the family home, the school nursery and both parents' workplaces were within very close proximity to one another (approximately a two-mile radius), making it

possible for the parents to manage coordination by themselves. The mother could also take advantage of flexitime work hours.

In two other cases, however, the same choices based on the quality of private nursery care and the additional educational input from the school nursery left the parents with very inconvenient provision, which they could not manage by themselves. In the lone-parent family, for example, the opening times of the private nursery were inconvenient and the mother relied on a neighbour in the mornings, but she also relied on up to three other people (and herself) to manage the lunchtime coordination point in order that her child could also attend school nursery. In the other case, the mother had to travel up to four miles across town in order for her child to attend the preferred private nursery, but she also wanted her child to receive nursery school education, which was situated close to the family home. Transporting the child between this provision could therefore involve a round trip of eight miles which could take up to an hour by car. She therefore had to rely on a complex mix of support from the father and her friends to manage this package of care. These complex cases contrast with the mother who used shared nanny care.

The mother who used the shared nanny chose this care because she believed it was:

- Convenient for her family's needs.
- Better socially for her child than using a childminder.
- Enabling the childcare to take place in the family home rather than the carer's home.

She therefore chose nanny care for the same reasons of quality of care, but like the other parents, she also chose to use school nursery because of the additional educational input. However, in her case the nanny also transported children across the different care settings. Moreover, as the nanny care took place in the family home, this reduced the number of different care settings and, as the home was in close proximity to the school nursery, the journey times were also reduced. This all served to simplify coordination. Some parents therefore ended up with complex coordination partly because of the choices they made about childcare, but also perhaps because of 'choices' for mothers to work full time.

Four of the mothers worked full time and three others were full-time students. For the three studying full time, this was a requirement of the course and they had no choice over their hours, although one stated that she would like to work part time in the future. For the other four, they all expressed a desire for part-time work, but said they could not afford to give up their full-time earnings. These parents therefore felt they had little choice over their working/studying hours and they had to manage by relying on others for support.

Overall, the degree of coordination complexity was partly due to choices over childcare, where some forms of provision did not provide support with managing the interface between care settings. This proved particularly problematic when school nursery and private nursery care were used in combination, as these were not linked in any way. In the final analysis, this exposes the institutional and structural separation between pre-school education provided in primary school settings and some forms of private childcare and work times. Arguably, therefore, coordination complexity existed because it was parents who were fitting around inconvenient childcare services, rather than services fitting around parents and children, but also because of full-time working hours. Implicitly, the choices made over working hours played a part in coordination complexity, in that parents had to rely on others for extra support.

strategies used by parents to manage daily points in a typical working week with no exceptional events. These strategies included negotiating numerous forms of support that were often disjointed, but which nevertheless had to be planned, organised and paid for, in order to provide a seamless childcare service for children that dovetailed together with parents' work commitments.

The factors that contributed to the ease or difficulty of managing coordination points were highlighted most clearly in the two case studies, and it was shown that the age of the youngest child and the choices parents made over types of childcare, pre-school education, and working hours were all influential. But so too was not having support with transporting children from a father. For example, the full-time working lone parent had to rely on more people for support with coordination points, than those who had three or four children in the family. This suggests that all these factors were more important than the number of children in the family. The interesting questions are: how did mothers who worked part time manage coordination points? What strategies did they use and how far did this inform their choices over working hours and was there a difference in strategies across socioeconomic groups (as indicated by residential area status)? These questions are explored in the next chapter.

Summary

This chapter has reviewed the childcare and work arrangements among the full-time working/ studying mothers. Exploring the concept of coordination points has shown how among just seven cases there is a complex and hidden network of individuals offering informal, formal and insurance type support that is often *additional* to full-time formal childcare. For example, six of the seven mothers used full-time formal childcare/education for their pre-school children, yet they also had to rely on informal or formal support to manage at least one coordination point in the day. It was also likely that other additional arrangements were in place for managing coordination in school holidays, but it was not possible to cover these in depth. This study has therefore only reviewed the

4

Coordinating childcare and part-time work

In the previous chapter, it was relatively simple to map the working hours of the mothers in the full-time group. They generally worked regular daytime hours, Monday to Friday. This is not the case for the part-time working mothers where there is far greater diversity in the number of working hours and the times of the day and week they occur. This chapter begins by setting out these more complex working hours and childcare arrangements. It then discusses the management strategies used for dealing with coordination points and the decisions mothers' made both in returning to work and over their working hours. First, the family characteristics of this group of mothers are described.

Family characteristics

Table 4.1 shows that there were 21 families in which mothers worked part time, of which 13 families lived in Area A and eight in Area B. The majority were married couples (19), with only one cohabiting couple and one lone-parent family. The majority had two children, but eight families had three or four children. Additionally, six families had two children of pre-school age and the remainder had one child of pre-school age (aged four or less). The average age of the children was six years (the same as in the full-time working group), but the age range was higher, with the oldest being aged 18 compared to just 14 years old in the full-time group. Five families had children from a past relationship living in the household, but only in the lone-parent case did the non-resident father provide any support with childcare.

Table 4.1: Family characteristics of part-time working mothers

	Number of families
Marital status	
Married	19
Cohabiting	1
Lone parent	1
Number of children in the family	
1	1
2	12
3	6
4	2
Number of children in the family aged four or less	
1	15
2	6
Number of families which include children from a previous relationship	5
Average age of children (range)	6 (1-18)
Number of families living in each area	
Area A (more affluent)	13
Area B (less affluent)	8
Total number of families	21

Working hours and childcare arrangements

Table 4.2 shows weekly childcare arrangements and mothers' working hours. While there were variations in the times of the day mothers worked, just over half (11 of the 21 cases) only worked office daytime hours between Monday and Friday. Of the rest, one mother worked only on a Saturday, five worked evenings only, two worked both day and evenings, one worked shifts (involving day, night and evening shifts) and one mother worked only during the night.

Table 4.2: Weekly childcare arrangements and mothers' working hours, part-time working mothers

Case number[a]	Mothers' total weekly work hours	Mothers' type of work hours	Latest time mothers' finish (f) start work (s)	Ages of all children in the family	Age of pre-school child	Private nursery	Childminder	Nanny	Grandparent (GP)/other	Fathers	School nursery	Total hours	Total number of types of care per family
A-01	21	Day	(f) 2.30pm	8, 5, 3	3	–	–	–	12.55	–	12.30	25.25	2
A-04	16	Day	(f) 5pm	4, 3	4	–	–	15.10	–	–	14.35	29.45	3
					3	8.30	–	21	–	–	n/a	29.30	
A-06	20	Day	(f) 1pm	6, 3	3	–	14.15	–	9.30	–	10	33.45	3
A-13	18.30	Day	(f) 3pm	6, 3	3	–	14.30	–	–	–	10	24.30	2
A-15	20	Day	(f) 12–1pm	6, 4	4	–	–	–	3 to 8	10	12.30	22.25 (max)	3
A-16	16	Day	(f) 4pm	4, 2	4	–	10	–	1.15	–	14.35	25.50	3
					2	–	15.30	–	4	–	n/a	19.30	
A-18	21	Day	(f) 5.30pm	4, 1	4	25.30	–	–	–	–	–	25.30	1
					1	25.30	–	–	–	–	n/a	25.30	
A-26	22	Day	(f) 5.30pm	8, 5, 4	4	–	–	19.55	–	–	12.30	27.15[b]	2[c]
B-11	4	Day (w/e)	(f) 4pm	3	3	–	–	–	4 GP/father share	GP/father share	12.30	16.30	3
B-14	27	Day	(f) 3pm	16, 12, 4	4	–	24.10	–	–	–	12.30	36.40	2
B-20	12	Day	(f) 6pm or later	4, 2	4	–	–	–	6	–	12.30	18.30	4
					2	–	6	–	–	6	n/a	12	
B-30	17	Day	(f) 4pm	15, 13, 3	3	–	23.15	–	–	–	n/a	23.15	1
A-12	11.20	Day/eve	(f) varies weekly	8, 6, 4, 2	4	–	–	–	–	11.20	12.30	23.50	3
					2	4.30	–	–	–	11.20	n/a	15.50	
B-21	16.45	Day/eve	(s) 5pm	18, 6, 2	2	–	–	–	16.45 Sibling/father share	–	n/a	16.45	2
A-08	22.30	Shifts	(f) varies daily	5, 4	4	–	36	–	–	–	12.30	48.30	2[c]

Hours of childcare for pre-school children (expressed in hours and minutes)

26

Table 4.2: continued

Case number[a]	Mothers' total weekly work hours	Mothers' type of work hours	Latest time mothers' (f) finish (s) start work	Ages of all children in the family	Age of pre-school child	Hours of childcare for pre-school children (expressed in hours and minutes)							Total number of types of care per family
						Private nursery	Childminder	Nanny	Grandparent (GP)/other	Fathers	School nursery	Total hours	
A-07	9	Evening	(s) 6pm	6, 4	4	–	–	–	–	9	14.35	29.50	2[d]
A-17	8 to 12	Evening	(s) 6 or 8 pm	8, 3	3	–	–	–	–	8 to 12	12.30	22.30 (max)	2
B-32	16	Evening	(s) 4pm	18, 15, 14, 3	3	–	–	–	10 Sibling/neighbour 6		12.30	28.30	4
B-35	20	Evening	(s) 4pm	4, 1	4	–	–	–	7.30 (+)	15.15 (–)	10	32.45	3
					1	–	–	–	7.30 (+)	15.15 (–)	n/a	22.45	
B-36	19.30	Evening	(s) 5pm	13, 8, 2	2	5	–	–	–	19.30	n/a	24.30	2
A-39	10	Night	(s) 6pm	7, 3	3	–	–	–	–	10	–	10	1
Total number types of care							4	7	2	6 (GP alone) 2 (Sibling + other) 1 (GP + other)	9 (Father alone)		16

Notes: [a] A = more affluent Area A; B = less affluent Area B.

[b] The numbers do not add up as there was an overlap in hours when the nanny was paid during the hours the child was in school nursery.

[c] These families also use after school care for their older children to cover mothers' working hours.

[d] This family used AFSC one day per week as mother attended FE one day per week.

(w/e) = works at weekend only.

(+) = Likely to provide more hours of childcare.

(–) = Likely to provide less hours of childcare.

The majority who worked atypical hours could also work at the weekends, but none worked every weekend.

Most importantly, these working patterns show that in 13 cases mothers' working hours were dovetailed around the school day. Either mothers finished work prior to the end of the school day[1] (five cases) or they started work after the school day finished, sometime between 4pm and 8pm (seven cases). This meant that in all 13 cases the parents had no need for formal AFSC for their school age children and did not use it. The mothers cared for the children immediately after school themselves (although one mother did use AFSC one day per week when she attended a training course). This low use of AFSC was surprising, especially as in nine of these 13 cases, the mothers had primary school aged children and could potentially make use of such a service. In the remaining seven cases[2], the mothers' working hours extended beyond the school day, which meant that they were not available to collect children from school. However, in only two of these cases did the mothers use AFSC, the rest had children who were too old (aged 13 and above) or too young (under five years old) for such care. In total therefore, only two out of the 21 used formal AFSC for their primary school aged children. There was, however, a much higher use of childcare services for pre-school children aged four years or less.

Weekly childcare arrangements and mothers' working hours for part-time working mothers

Table 4.2 shows that the most common form of childcare for pre-school children was free school nursery. Sixteen out of a possible 18 used school nursery where children were aged between three and four years old and thus of an eligible age[3]. Therefore, in only two cases was it not used, even though the children were eligible.

The next most common form of care was that provided by fathers. Eleven fathers provided care, but in two cases this was shared between the father and either a grandparent or an older sibling. This was followed by childminder care (seven cases), grandparent care (six cases), private nursery care (four cases), nanny care (two cases) and shared care between an older sibling and a neighbour (one case). The picture of care, however, is more complex than this.

While free school nursery was most commonly used, the mothers' working hours did not always correspond with this care. Only three mothers worked during all the hours their children were in school nursery, and a further seven worked only some of these hours (not shown). Moreover, of the four cases using private nurseries, three mothers said this was to give them a break from both work and parenting and was not used to cover working hours. It seemed, therefore, that school nursery and private nursery were not always utilised as childcare while mothers were at work. However, nearly half (10) used formal fee-paying care such as a childminder, nanny or a private nursery (one case only) to cover the mothers' working hours.

Even though there was a complex mix of care, two patterns emerged: the 12 mothers who worked daytime office type hours (cases A-01 to B-30) tended to use private fee-paying care (nine cases) and occasionally this was combined with some family care. These mothers' working hours were also more likely to partially correspond with free school nursery times. The nine mothers who worked evenings and night shifts (cases A-12 to A-39) tended to rely on free family care and obviously would not be at work when their children were attending school nursery. One reason for using family care in the evenings is because there is rarely any formal care available. In addition, if these two patterns of care and working hours are examined in relation to socioeconomic status (as represented by whether families lived in Area A [more affluent] or Area B [less affluent]), then most of the potentially more affluent mothers (eight of the 13 living in Area A) worked daytime rather than evening hours. This might mean that more mothers in Area A could afford to pay for formal childcare and therefore could 'choose' to work during the daytime. These patterns imply some element of choice over working hours that are matched to childcare (discussed on page 36), but

---

[1]   Approximately before 3-3.30pm.

[2]   This excludes the case where the mother worked Saturdays only.

[3]   To be eligible, children have to be aged between three and four years old. In some cases where the children were aged three they were waiting to start nursery in the forthcoming term.

Table 4.3: Number of daily coordination points managed by families in a typical week

Two coordination points	Three coordination points	Four coordination points	Five coordination points[a]
3	11	5	2

Note: [a] In these two families the additional fifth coordination point only occurred weekly.

also they raise questions about the number of coordination points faced by these parents.

Coordination points

As was the case for full-time working mothers, five coordination points in the day were identified, although the late evening point was replaced with a mid-evening point, reflecting the evening working hours of the part-time group (see Figure 4.1). The most common number of coordination points to be managed daily was three and the least common was five (this fifth point tended to occur weekly rather than daily) (see Table 4.3).

The strategies used by part-time working mothers were similar to the full-time working mothers, involving arranging regular informal and formal support. However, the strategy of arranging back-up support was slightly different.

Management strategies

Arranging regular informal support with coordination points

Table 4.4 shows the number of people providing informal support in each case in a typical working week. Unlike the full-time working mothers, however, not all the part-time workers relied on informal support from someone else for at least one coordination point in a day, only 10 did. Even so, of the 11 mothers who did not receive informal support, three did use formal support (also shown in Table 4.4).

Fathers most commonly provided support; eight helped to transport children across settings for at least one of the coordination points and in three of those the fathers also provided wrap-around care in the evenings. A further five fathers provided wrap-around care in the evenings/ weekends, but were not involved in transporting children (at the evening coordination points).

Thus, eight fathers provided evening wrap-around care and this compared to only one father in the full-time group (most full-time working mothers were home in the evenings).

Grandparents (five cases) and other family/ friends (three cases) also helped with transporting children at coordination points. While in another four cases, grandparents or other family/friends provided wrap-around care in the evenings.

In total, 38 people were involved in providing informal support by transporting children to and from settings at coordination points: 21 mothers, eight fathers and nine grandparents/family or friends.

Overall, the majority of mothers relied on informal support, but the pattern varied depending on the coordination point in the day:

- Morning point – fathers provided most support (six).
- Lunchtime point – this resulted from school nursery provision and all but five families used this care. Grandparents provided most support (five) and there was none at all from friends.
- Post-school point – this was relevant to all but three cases (the children in the family were too young for school). Only one mother relied on informal support (though some relied on formal support, see Table 4.4).
- Early evening point – only two mothers relied on informal support, both provided by fathers (although many fathers did provide wrap-around care).
- Mid-evening point – only wrap-around care was provided at this point by two fathers.

The low use of informal support around the post-school coordination point reflected how mothers' employment was dovetailed around the school day, leaving them free to collect the children themselves. Importantly, some mothers also relied on formal support with coordination points (see Table 4.4).

Figure 4.1: Model of coordination points for part-time working mothers in a typical working week

Daily points

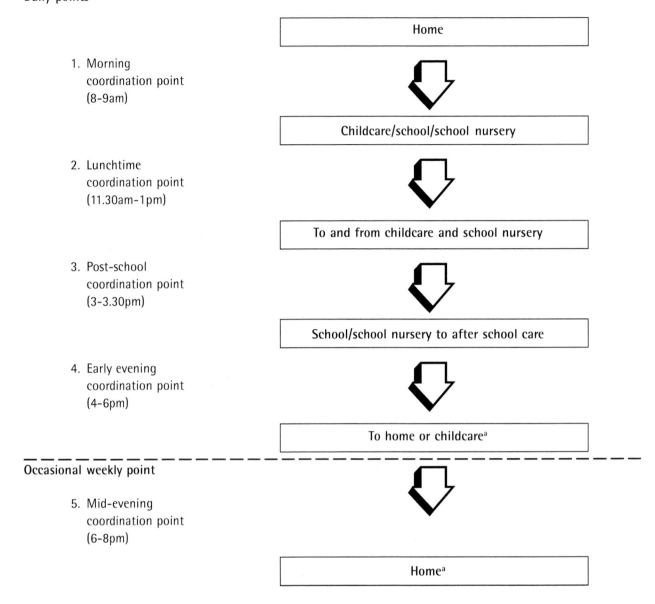

1. Morning coordination point (8-9am)

Home

2. Lunchtime coordination point (11.30am-1pm)

Childcare/school/school nursery

3. Post-school coordination point (3-3.30pm)

To and from childcare and school nursery

4. Early evening coordination point (4-6pm)

School/school nursery to after school care

To home or childcare[a]

Occasional weekly point

5. Mid-evening coordination point (6-8pm)

Home[a]

Note: [a] One child went from AFSC to further childminder care one evening per week until the father picked him up sometime after 7pm or the mother did at around 8pm after finishing work.

Arranging regular formal support with coordination points

Table 4.4 also shows the formal support received with coordination points. This was mostly confined to mothers who worked during the day, with none of those working evenings using formal support. However, up to 12 childminders[4] or nannies commonly transported children at the morning, lunchtime or post-school coordination points. In only one case did the childminder not

help in this way, but only at the morning coordination point. Childminders' husbands could also provide support by transporting children to and from school nursery at lunchtime. Childminders and nannies were valuable not only in terms of providing childcare, but also in transporting children. They were pivotal in supporting parents who worked during the day with the interface between home – school – school nursery – childcare. This highlights their flexibility and contrasts with the inflexibility of private nurseries found among the full-time working group. In the full-time group, mothers

---

[4] Including childminders' husbands.

Table 4.4: Persons providing informal and [formal] support with daily coordination points in a typical working week

Case number[a]	Ages of children	Mothers' type of working hours[b]	Daily coordination points					Total people helping with coordination points[b]	
			Morning 8–9am	Lunchtime 11.30am–1.30pm	Post-school 3–3.30pm	Early evening 4–6pm	Mid evening 6–9pm	[Formal]	Informal
A–01	8, 5, 3	Day (f) 2.30pm	Mother	Mother Maternal grandparent Paternal grandparent	Mother (Grandparent as back-up)	–	–	0	3
A–04	4, 3	Day (f) 5pm	Mother [Two nannies]	Mother (Friend as back-up) [Two nannies]	n/a	Mother	–	2	1
A–06	6, 3	Day (f) 1pm	Mother Friend Grandparent[d]	Grandparent [Childminder] [Childminder's husband]	Mother	–	–	2	3
A–13	6, 3	Day (f) 3pm	Mother [Childminder]	Mother [Childminder]	Mother [Childminder]	–	–	1	1
A–15	6, 4	Day (f) 12–1pm	Mother	Father Aunt	Mother	–	–	0	3
A–16	4, 2	Day (f) 4pm	Mother GP [Childminder]	Mother Grandparent [Childminder's husband]	n/a	Mother Father	–	2	3
A–18	4, 1	Day (f) 5.30pm	Mother	n/a	n/a	Mother (Grandparent as back-up)	–	0	1
A–26	8, 5, 4	Day (f) 5.30pm	Mother [Nanny]	Mother [Nanny]	Mother [Nanny]	Mother	–	1	1
B–11	3	Day (w/e)	n/a	Mother	Mother	–	–	0	1
B–14	16, 12, 4	Day (f) 3pm	Father [Childminder]	– [Childminder]	Mother	–	–	1	2
B–20	4, 2	Day (f) 6pm varies	Father Mother [Childminder]	Grandparent [Childminder]	Mother [Childminder]	Mother	–	1	3

Table 4.4: continued

Case number[a]	Ages of children	Mothers' type of working hours[b]	Daily coordination points					Total people helping with coordination points[b]	
			Morning 8–9am	Lunchtime 11.30am–1.30pm	Post-school 3–3.30pm	Early evening 4–6pm	Mid evening 6–9pm	[Formal]	Informal
B-30	15, 13, 3	Day (f) 4pm	Mother	n/a	–	Mother	–	0	1
A-08	5, 4	Shifts (f) varies	Father [Childminder] [Out of school club]	– [Childminder]	– [AFSC]	Mother Father [2 childminders]	Father[e]	4	2
A-12	8, 6, 4, 2	Day/eve (f) varies	Mother Father	Mother Father Grandparent	Mother Father Grandparent Friend	–	–	0	4
B-21	18, 6, 2	Day/eve (s) 5pm	Mother	n/a	Mother	Sibling[e] Father[e]	–	0	1
A-07	6, 4	Evening (s) 6pm	Mother	Mother	Mother	Father[e] Friend[e]	–	0	1
A-17	8, 3	Evening (s) 6 or 8pm	Mother	Mother	Mother	Father[e]	Father[e]	0	1
B-32	18, 15, 14, 3	Evening (s) 4pm	Mother	Mother	Mother	Father[e] Sibling[e] Neighbour[e]	–	0	1
B-35	4, 1	Evening (s) 4pm	Mother	Mother	Mother	Grandparent[e] Father[e]	–	0	1
B-36	13, 8, 2	Evening (s) 5pm	Father	n/a	Mother	Father[e]	–	0	2
A-39	7, 3	Night (s) 6pm	Mother Father	– –	Mother	Father[e]	–	0	2
Total people (including mothers and fathers)			35	29	23	11	0	14	38

Notes: [a] A = more affluent Area A; B = less affluent Area B. [b] f = finish time; s = start time. [c] Including mothers and fathers.
[d] = A childminder provides childcare, but does not help with transporting children at this coordination point.
[e] = Wrap-around care provided, but not help with transporting children to and from different settings.

and occasionally fathers had to take time off work and/or rely on informal support to manage coordination points, particularly the lunchtime point when school nursery was used.

The use of formal and informal support and socioeconomic status

When the socioeconomic status of families is considered, those in the more affluent Area A used more support. Of the 13 families in Area A, the majority (10) used either formal or informal support (excluding mothers but including fathers [five]), and of those 10, seven of the mothers worked during the day. In other words, of the eight mothers in Area A who worked during the day, only one managed without any support from others with coordination points (A-18). Even so, this mother (A-18) did feel the need to have back-up support from a grandparent.

In comparison, among the eight families living in Area B, only three used formal or informal support (excluding mothers but including fathers [three]) with coordination points, and of those, two mothers worked during the day. Remember overall, that among the eight living in Area B, four mothers worked during the day and four worked during the evening. This suggests a complex mix of factors in relation to coordination, in that lower income families seemed to be more self-reliant in transporting children except, that is, if the mothers worked during the day.

The use of formal and informal support and numbers of children

It could be expected that families with greater numbers of children might use more support from others with coordination points. Yet, this does not appear to be the case. Table 4.4 shows that the family which had the greatest numbers of people involved with coordination points (A-08) only had two children. They were also the family with the most complex arrangements (as discussed on page 34 – case study three). This complexity was related more to other factors such as working hours and the distance between care settings, rather than the number of children. Similarly, it was not the case that families who were the most self-reliant with coordination points all had fewer children; of the eight who

used no support, four had two children, two had three children and one family had four children.

Arranging insurance back-up support

There were major differences in back-up support strategies used by the part-time working mothers compared to those working full-time. Part-time mothers gave much less weight to nurturing reciprocal relationships with friends to provide back-up support. Indeed, in only two cases did mothers discuss this as being important. It is hard to say what the reasons for this might be. It could be that as more part-time mothers worked evenings, they were more reliant on fathers to provide wrap-around care and therefore had less need for back-up support from friends/ neighbours. This reliance on fathers is given further weight by the strategy adopted by the one working lone parent. She intentionally employed her childminder for longer hours than strictly necessary as back-up care 'in case' she was delayed at work. It seems that confining working hours to evenings and weekends was in itself a management strategy that allowed mothers (or at least partnered mothers) to be free to manage coordination points unaided and without the need for back-up support from anyone other than fathers (as shown in Table 4.4).

More commonly, the part-time working mothers were concerned with back-up support in the event of children becoming sick. Six mothers discussed having support from family or friends in such an event, including, in one case, support from the non-resident father. In a further three cases, the mothers regularly paid childminders as back-up nursing care for school aged children who might become sick. In a further case the mother deliberately ran up extra flexitime hours so she could come home 'in an emergency'.

The picture that emerges of coordination points is one where the least complex arrangements were found among mothers whose part-time work was confined to the evenings or weekends. In these circumstances, the parents were generally self-sufficient and managed both the childcare and coordination points by themselves, with fathers playing a major role in providing wrap-around care. In contrast, the most complex arrangements were found among the mothers whose part-time work occurred during the day.

In these circumstances, parents tended to rely on more support from others with coordination points. It is hard to be sure about the effect of socioeconomic status. Similar numbers of fathers in Area A and Area B provided wrap-around care in the evenings while the mothers worked. Overall, however, the more affluent families in Area A tended to use more support with coordination points; 10 out of 13 compared to only three out of eight families living in Area B. Having more children in the family, on its own, did not seem to make coordination more complex. Given this evidence, it is possible that making a choice for mothers to only work atypical hours (rather than to just work part-time)

could be a management strategy used in its own right to reduce coordination complexity. This is exemplified further in case study three.

Complex management of coordination points

Case study three (A-08) highlights the most complex management of coordination points among the part-time working group and is directly related to the mothers' shift hours (only one mother worked these kind of shifts). The evening coordination point was the most complex, though this tended to occur on a weekly rather than a daily basis. As will be

Case study three: Complex management of coordination points

The complexity of this family's childcare arrangements occurred at the time of the interview and reflected both the father's long hours and the mother's shift hours. The father worked over 50 hours per week and the mother's shifts involved starting work prior to school opening hours and also working one night a week until 9pm (a total of 22 hours). They had two children aged four and five years. Childcare services included: using a breakfast and after school club (oldest child); school nursery part-time (youngest child); one childminder to provide coordination support and wrap-around care for both children; and another childminder to only provide coordination support. The father also provided coordination support and wrap-around care in the late evenings. Excluding maternal care, six types of childcare were required on a weekly basis, the highest number among part-time working mothers.

At the *morning coordination point*, the father always took the oldest child to the breakfast club within the school, as his workplace was close by. When the mother was working early he would also take the youngest child to the childminder. The childminder would then take the youngest child to school nursery for 9am. The father's journey by car took about 30 minutes if dropping off one child but up to an hour if dropping off both children. Therefore, three sets of care were required to deal with the morning coordination point and provide wrap-around care when the mother worked early. Otherwise, when the mother was not working or working late, the childminder was not used in the morning.

At the *lunchtime coordination point*, when the mother was at work, the childminder collected the youngest child from school nursery and provided wrap-around care until one of the parents finished work in the afternoon or evening. The older child remained in school.

At the *post-school coordination point*, when the mother was working late, the older child attended an after school club within his primary school (the younger child being cared for by the childminder). Otherwise, the mother would collect him directly from school (and she would care for the younger child).

At the *early and mid-evening coordination points*, when the mother worked late, the father would collect the oldest child from the AFSC at around 5.30-6pm and take him to his workplace. The childminder, who was looking after the youngest child in her home (and other people's children), would then drive to the fathers' workplace to pick up the older child and provide wrap-around care in her home for both children until the father finished work at around 7pm. The father would then collect both children from the childminders mid-evening, take them home and provide further wrap-around care. In order for the childminder to provide this pick up service for the oldest child early evening, a second childminder was employed for an hour to care for all the other children left in the first childminder's home. The parents' paid for this second childminder and also for petrol costs. Four sets of care were therefore involved in providing support with coordination points and wrap-around care on the evening the mother worked late.

shown, it is highly unlikely that the strategies for managing the evening coordination points could have been adopted daily, at least, not without causing considerable stress to all involved.

Case study three illustrates the difficulties this family faced as a result of both parents' working hours. However, the complexity of care in the evenings had occurred only in the last year as a result of the mother changing from working fixed hours five days a week to working shifts over fewer days. The mother instigated this because the oldest child started primary school and she said she wanted to 'be there' to take him to and from school herself. Despite the complexity, the mother said she found the arrangements OK and that her childminder was fantastic. However, she also said that it put the father under more stress when he had responsibility for collecting the children. Despite this, she wanted to keep arrangements as they were, perhaps because it satisfied her desire to be there for her child. There were two other contrary examples, however, where changes were made in the mothers' working hours to specifically simplify coordination and reduce stress.

Instigating change to reduce coordination complexity

In the first example case (A-04), the mother wanted to reduce the number of carers who helped with childcare and with coordination points (five in total), one of whom was employed for just an hour a day to collect and care for the oldest child from school nursery at lunchtime. She therefore reduced her working hours from four days to two days per week[5]. As she said:

> "I had to stop that [using so many carers] because it was just ridiculous, you know he [oldest child] was just with too many people, so I didn't work Thursday and Fridays because it just got silly." (Mother of two children aged four and three years)

In the second example case (A-17), the mother wanted to reduce the stress involved in 'running back and forth' to pick up children from various

care settings and so she changed her hours from daytime to evenings only. As she said:

> "I thought this is no good, we are just running around in circles, it was so hard. I know it doesn't sound an awful lot, just picking them up and running back and forth, and she [youngest child] was not a settled child and still isn't and then I decided to, you know, cut it down to the evening work." (Mother of two children aged eight and three years)

Overall, case study three and the two examples demonstrate a number of important points:

- Managing coordination points could be even more complex for part-time working mothers than for full-time working mothers, particularly where they worked during the day.
- It was not the numbers of children in the family that made coordination complex; in each of the three most complex cases the families had only two children.
- Instigating change in the mothers' working hours was a strategy used to minimise coordination complexity.
- Instigating change in the mothers' working hours was a strategy used to address the needs of children and also mothers' needs to 'be there' for children.
- Restricting mothers' employment to 'atypical hours' could be a strategy used to minimise the number of care settings for children and thereby reduce coordination complexity.

Other part-time working mothers also expressed the need to 'be there' and it was interlinked with decisions about both returning to work and to choices over working hours.

Decisions to return to work

While all these mothers were working part time at the time of the interview, many had managed to have a few years free from paid work when their children were of pre-school age. Indeed, only five mothers were currently in the same jobs they had prior to having children, although they were now working part time. A further two mothers had been in continuous employment since having children, but had changed their jobs but not their occupations as nurses. Continuous

---

[5] This mother went on to temporarily give up work for other reasons, discussed in the next section.

employment therefore occurred in only seven of the 21 cases. Thus, it was more common for mothers to experience changes in employment over time, but it was not possible to accurately track these changes for individual cases. What can be identified, however, are drivers to change at two points in time, first in terms of returning to work after starting a family and second in terms of making changes to the number and type of hours spent in employment.

Financial drivers

Financial needs were important drivers in mothers' decisions to return to paid work. However, this was not always the main driver. Only five mothers said they 'had to go back to work' for financial reasons, while 11 said it was only part of the reason for returning. Another five mothers said they felt fortunate that they did not need to work for financial reasons; four of them were married to men in professional/managerial occupations and these four women were also in professional occupations. Of the 21 mothers, only six were currently in professional/managerial occupations, the remainder worked in administration or the retail/catering industry. For nearly all mothers, however, going back to work represented something more than simply earning money.

Stimulation drivers

Seven mothers described their decision to go back to work in terms of escaping some kind of 'madness' or 'death' induced by being at home alone with children. They used language like 'going mad' at home, going 'stir crazy' or 'crazy', going 'gaga' or they described how they were 'just dying' at home or that their 'brain was atrophying'. Five mothers stressed how returning to work was important in social terms. They wanted to be stimulated by 'adult company', with one mother even saying that her 'work was her social life'. Six other mothers simply talked about the enjoyment or fulfilment they got from doing paid work. Despite or because of these advantages, only two of the 21 mothers said they would prefer to be at home and would give up work if they did not need the money.

Going back to paid work was therefore not always an easy or straightforward 'choice'.

Indeed, some expressed ambivalence about returning and said they were upset about leaving their child. One reluctant mother said that she only returned initially because otherwise she would have had to repay her maternity pay. Others said they went back mainly because their employers asked them and others because they had free childcare in the form of grandparent support. There was, therefore, a range of push and pull factors that encouraged returning to work and these could occur at different times in the mothers' lives. Importantly, however, it seemed that choosing to work part time as opposed to full time was related to a number of other interrelated factors.

Choices over working hours

Children's health and well-being

Three mothers implied that they were forced to alter their sense of 'priorities' about work and being a mother after one of their children experienced health or behavioural problems. This resulted in two of the mothers reducing their working hours. They described their experiences thus:

First family:

"... the best thing I ever did was handing in my resignation – because it changed the way I looked at work and that was critically important to me. I needed to stop wanting to be a full-time worker and instead be a worker and a mum." (Mother of two children, changed from full-time to part-time work, to temporarily stopping work)

Second family:

"... well I was doing six days a week ... and he [youngest child] was just getting fretful and you know, clinging to me all the time and getting upset, and I thought, well you're just missing out on him, you know, then you bring him home and then you put him to bed, so you know, you're missing out on them a lot ... and he was, he kept lashing out at everybody, hitting everybody all the time and really acting funny so we decided to find a job that would fit round [husband's] work." (Mother of three children, changed from full-time day to part-time evening work)

Third family:

"It's only since I've had [second child] that even the possibility that I might want to stop work has occurred to me.... It just makes you, something like that [child's ill health] always makes you readjust your priorities." (Mother of two children, worked daytime hours and did not change them)

It seems the health and well-being of individual children altered these mothers' perspectives on their role as workers. In two families this acted as a driver to change mothers' working hours. This driver, however, was not as clear-cut as the children's health/behavioural problems might suggest; there were other underlying reasons. In the first family this included three interlinked factors: first, the mother said that her employer was extremely non-family friendly; second, a change in her husband's employment meant that he could not help share the care responsibilities; and third, there was a complex childcare package that became unmanageable. In the second family, there was one main reason. The mother had worked full time with her oldest child and believed that she had 'missed out' watching him grow up, she was not prepared to do that again with her youngest child who seemed to exhibit behavioural problems as a result of his mother's absence.

Individual children's needs

While in the previous three families the children had fairly serious health/behavioural problems, apparently lesser problems among specific children in the family could also affect mothers' choices over working hours. For example, another three mothers described how some of the children in their family were 'different' and that they needed their mothers to spend more time with them. These specific children either did not sleep well, were described as more boisterous than other children in the family, or were described as 'clingy', meaning that they got very distressed if the mother left them. Partly in response to this different behaviour, one mother reduced her working hours by half, another changed her hours from daytime to work

evenings only and another deliberately chose to return to work evenings only. Clearly the real and/or perceived needs of individual children could affect mothers' working behaviour, both in terms of the amount of hours they worked and/or the times of the day/week in which they worked, although this was often intermingled with other factors (discussed on p 38).

Having more than one child

Apart from the perceived needs of individual children, simply having more children also acted as a driver to change working hours. In this instance, however, change was closely tied to childcare costs. Three mothers cited the rising cost of formal childcare associated with having second or third children as a reason for temporarily giving up paid work or changing their hours of employment to evenings/ weekends when the children would be in the care of their fathers. Two others said that formal childcare was not an option when they had more than one child and that the only reason they could work at all was because of free childcare provided by grandparents. Another mother said that after having her second child the increase in childcare costs meant it was financially not worthwhile working, but she continued to work because she enjoyed it and in the long term it would eventually pay when her youngest child started school. Some mothers therefore responded to the rising costs of formal childcare associated with having more children by temporarily stopping work or by changing the hours of employment to work atypical hours and/or by relying on free childcare provided by grandparents, or by tolerating the high costs of childcare in the short term to gain in the long run when children started school. However, a more general theme emerged from the data that specifically explained why some mothers chose to restrict their hours of work to specific times of the day/week, irrespective of other factors.

'Being there'

The theme that explained choices to work restricted hours[6] was where mothers expressed a desire to 'be there' for children and/or where they did not want to 'miss out' watching them grow up. The underlying reasons for these sentiments were difficult to pin down clearly, but involved one or more of the following factors:

- A desire to 'be there' to collect older children from school – this was seen as a particularly important time for mothers to be present (five cases).
- A feeling of having 'missed' their own mothers as children because she had worked, or conversely feeling they had not 'missed out' because their own mothers were 'always there' and had not worked (four cases).
- A feeling of having 'missed out' watching older children in the family grow up due to having worked full time and/or daytime in the past (three cases).
- A sense of treating all children in the family equally – that it was not fair on younger children to work during the day when the mother had 'been there' for older children when they were young (two cases).
- Wanting to 'be there' and care for their children 'totally' by themselves (two cases).
- Having a 'late child' in a second relationship where the mother (and father) wanted to 'enjoy' being with that child and spend as much time as possible with them (one case).

Making a choice to work part time therefore involved a range of factors including: practical considerations in terms of reducing childcare costs when there was more than one child in the family; perceptions of children's needs for their mothers because of fairly serious health/ behavioural problems and/or because of the personality of an individual child; and/or because of perceptions that children needed their mothers or fathers to pick them up and 'be there' for them after school.

---

[6] Restricted hours is very similar but not synonymous with 'atypical hours'; it refers to the choices made to restrict the hours of maternal employment to the times when children were either at school (school hours) or when another parent/grandparent was available to provide childcare (evenings, weekends or night shifts = atypical hours).

Summary

This chapter has described the childcare arrangements, working hours, coordination points and management strategies used by 21 part-time working mothers. The main features to emphasise are:

- Childcare and working hours were more complex for part-time working mothers than for full-time working mothers.
- Two broad patterns of mothers' working hours emerged:
  ‣ hours 'overlapping' with the end of the school day;
  ‣ hours 'dovetailing' around the end of the school day (working pre- or post-school finish times).
- The majority of families (13) received informal or formal support with coordination points.
- Some 31 people (excluding mothers, but including fathers/others) could be involved in transporting children in a typical working week.
- Formal support with coordination points (from childminders, nannies or AFSC) was confined to those who worked daytime hours (sometime between 8am-5.30pm).
- School nursery was the most common form of care, but was not always used to cover all the mothers' working hours.
- Fathers were the main child carers after school nursery. They mainly provided wrap-around care in the evenings.

The picture that emerges is that the least complex arrangements were confined to those mothers who worked atypical evening/weekend hours. Parents, particularly mothers, managed the childcare and coordination points by themselves, with fathers also playing a major role in providing wrap-around care in the evenings.

Interestingly, the number of children in the family did not, on its own, seem to make coordination more complex. Possibly this is because where there are two, three or four children in the family of primary school age they would all be attending the same school[7]. Thus,

---

[7] Older children in the family could be attending secondary school, but they may be able to travel on their own and therefore do not add to the coordination complexity.

there would be only one journey and one care setting for all of them. Coordination complexity does not therefore necessarily rise in direct relationship with the number of children. What seems more important is the age of the children and the gap between them. For example, having one child of pre-school age and one of primary school age is as complex to manage as having one child of pre-school age and three of primary school age (assuming that all three older ones go to the same primary school). Therefore, it is likely that one of the factors increasing coordination complexity is having children of both pre-school and school age in the family.

In relation to socioeconomic status, although the families in the richer Area A used more support from others with coordination points (including fathers, but excluding mothers), childcare and coordination appeared much more complex for families where the mother worked during the day, regardless of whether they lived in Area A or B. It is likely that coordination complexity is interrelated with 'choices' to work during the day or evening. This was exemplified most clearly in case study three where the mother worked shift hours and in the two cases where the mothers changed their working hours to reduce coordination complexity. However, there were other reasons for changing working hours and for choosing part-time employment.

Financial and stimulation needs underpinned many decisions to return to work in the first instance, but making a decision to work only part time involved different factors. A couple of mothers reduced their working hours from full time in response to children's health needs, while a few others chose to work part time as they believed that individual children in the family were 'different' and needed to spend more time with their mothers. Having more children was another reason for reducing working hours, although this was often closely tied to childcare costs. Some mothers changed their hours of employment to work only atypical hours to reduce childcare costs after having second or third children, while others with more than one child highlighted how they could not have worked at all without the free help provided by grandparents. It has been argued that the reason why part-time work among mothers in the UK is so common is due to a lack of suitable and affordable childcare (Crompton, 1997, p 35; Dex, 1999, p 36). Certainly, many of these mothers

did not use formal fee-paying childcare to cover their working hours (11 cases – see Table 4.2). Thus, choosing to work part time in the evenings/weekends to take advantage of the free care provided by fathers/relatives potentially made combining work and family life more feasible and economically viable. However, the 'choice' to work part time among these mothers was commonly expressed in terms of needing to 'be there' for children, particularly after school, or not wanting to 'miss out' watching their children grow up. Coordination problems did play an explicit part in a few mothers' choices to change their working hours, but this was less common. However, this could simply reflect the success of the management strategies that were being adopted in arranging formal and informal support with coordination points and/or in the choice made by mothers to work only evenings or atypical hours. It could be that non-working mothers faced greater problems with coordination because they could not arrange support with coordination points when in employment. This is explored further in the next chapter.

5

Non-working mothers' choices over employment

This chapter outlines the non-working mothers' childcare arrangements and strategies for managing coordination points. An analysis of previous employment patterns is presented, which considers what kinds of factors influenced these mothers' decisions to stop paid work in the past. It then discusses how much coordinating childcare and work commitments acts as a potential barrier to returning to work in the immediate future.

Family characteristics

There were 12 families in which mothers did not do paid work at the time of the interview. As might be expected, the majority (eight) lived in the less affluent Area B and the majority of the lone parents in the whole sample (four out of six) were in this non-working group[1] and they all lived in Area B. The marital status of the rest included six married and two cohabiting couples. The children were on average older, aged nine compared to aged six in both the working groups (see Tables 3.1 and 4.1). The family size was quite large, with five families having three or four children. Additionally, proportionally more families had two children of pre-school age; half in this non-working group compared to six out of 21 in the part-time workers group and none in the full-time working group.

Table 5.1: Family characteristics of non-working mothers

	Number of families
Marital status	
Married	6
Cohabiting	2
Lone parent	4
Number of children in the family	
1	1
2	6
3	2
4	3
Number of children in the family aged four or less	
1	6
2	6
Number of families which include children from a previous relationship	2
Number of families living in the two areas	
Area A (more affluent)	4
Area B (less affluent)	8
Average age of children (range)	9 (1-13)
Total number of families	12

Childcare

Table 5.2 shows the childcare arrangements for the non-working mothers and, as might be expected, they used very little formal childcare for their pre-school age children, apart from nursery education (eight cases). Table 5.2 also shows that one mother did use private nursery care and another used specialised childcare services in the form of a family centre and a family support worker. None used AFSC for their school age children.

---

[1] All four of the lone parents were dependent on Income Support benefit.

Table 5.2: Weekly childcare arrangements for non-working mothers

| Case number[a] | Ages of all children in the family | Age of pre-school children | Hours of childcare for pre-school children (expressed in hours and minutes) | | | |
			Private nursery	Other	School nursery	Total weekly hours pre-school childcare
A-19	4, 1	4			14.35	14.35
		1			n/a	
A-22	4, 3	4			12.30	12.30
		3			–	
A-27	1	1	9		n/a	9
A-28	6, 3, 1	3			12.30	12.30
		1			n/a	
B-09	8, 6, 4, 2	4			12.30	12.30
		2			n/a	
B-10	4, 2	4			12.30	12.30
		2			n/a	
B-23[b]	12, 9, 7, 3	3			12.30	12.30
B-24[b]	5, 3	3			10	10
B-31	10, 8, 3	3			–	
B-34[b]	13, 12, 7, 4	4			14.35	14.35
B-37[b]	5, 2	2			n/a	
B-40	2, 1	2		9	n/a	9
		1		3	n/a	3

Notes: [a] A = more affluent Area A; B = less affluent Area B.
[b] Lone-parent family.
n/a = children in family too young or old for AFSC.

This more restricted use of childcare services was reflected in the number of coordination points faced by these parents.

Coordination points

For the group as a whole, four coordination points were identified and, unlike the working mothers, there was no mid or late evening coordination point. In addition, the early evening point was only relevant to one case using private nursery care two afternoons a week finishing at 5.30pm (see Figure 5.1).

Thus, six mothers had to manage three daily coordination points: morning for school/school nursery, lunchtime to pick up or drop off at school nursery and post-school to pick up from school/school nursery. Five mothers had to manage only two coordination points in the day. The remaining mother had specialised childcare services that were managed by others and she therefore had no daily coordination points (see Table 5.3).

Figure 5.1: Model of coordination points for non-working mothers in a typical week

Daily points

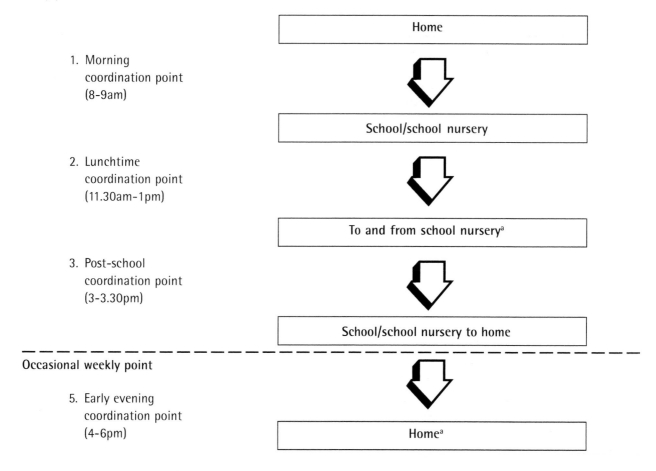

1. Morning
   coordination point
   (8-9am)

    Home

    School/school nursery

2. Lunchtime
   coordination point
   (11.30am-1pm)

    To and from school nursery[a]

3. Post-school
   coordination point
   (3-3.30pm)

    School/school nursery to home

Occasional weekly point

5. Early evening
   coordination point
   (4-6pm)

    Home[a]

Note: [a] One child went to a private nursery in the afternoon from 1pm-5.30pm two days per week.

None of these mothers faced difficulties with coordination points because they tended to take sole responsibility for dropping off and collecting children (although one non-resident father did collect his oldest child from school every Friday). Managing coordination points was therefore relatively easy in comparison to the working mothers. However, although none of these mothers were currently working, this did not mean that they had all remained out of employment continuously since having children and the evidence shows that coordination problems had occurred in the past.

Reasons for giving up work

Some mothers gave up work immediately after having their first child and had not yet returned, while others had returned for a short time but gave up later. In order to explore decisions at these different points in time, the non-working mothers were split into two groups – those who had not yet returned and those who had previously returned.

Table 5.3: Number of daily coordination points managed by families in a typical week[a]

Two coordination points	Three coordination points
5	6

Note: [a] Social services managed the coordination points in one case.

Non-returnees

Six mothers had never returned to paid work. Time spent out of employment ranged from two to eight years, but most commonly it was four years (three cases). Four of these mothers had previously worked in professional/managerial occupations. In the remaining two cases, one woman had been a teenage mother at age 16 and went on to have four children and had never worked. The other mother had only ever worked in unskilled part-time employment prior to having children. Despite these differences in employment experience, all six expressed strong beliefs that mothers should be at home full time, at least for the period when children were of pre-school age (three fathers were said to hold the same beliefs). Indeed, all five who had worked prior to becoming mothers said they had 'chosen' to give up work to be at home with their children. However, three mothers who had been in professional occupations also said their jobs were 'very stressful' and that they wanted a break. Even so, two of these mothers were now thinking of returning to work, despite having children of pre-school age, but not to the same jobs they had left. These two mothers were distinguished from the rest because they were actively looking for jobs, whereas the other four were deliberately postponing returning to work, at least until all their children were in school.

Overall, the reasons for not returning to work included:

- wanting to be a full-time mother;
- wanting a break from stressful jobs;
- never having worked prior to having children.

The other six mothers had all previously returned to work at some point after starting a family. In three cases they had returned to their previous job immediately after the birth of their first child, but for various reasons had given it up, while the other three mothers had returned to work later on. To explore this time dimension further, these six mothers will be split into two groups: immediate returnees and late returnees.

Immediate returnees

The three mothers who immediately returned to their previous jobs after the birth of their first

child described different but multiple reasons for giving up their jobs.

One mother had worked part time for three years and gave up her job when she had her second child. There were two main reasons: first, because she felt that it would be 'too much of a burden' to ask the grandparents to look after two children; and second, her job disappeared as a result of her employer selling the small business when she realised the mother might not return to work.

Another mother had worked part time for 18 months and gave up work following a miscarriage. She believed that she would not have any more children and said she therefore wanted to be at home with her child and to 'enjoy him'. However, she also gave up work because the job was 'very stressful' and she had to travel over 40 miles, resulting in long 12-hour working days. Consequently, she got 'fed up juggling' work and caring and felt she was not doing either job very well and she feared her child was 'missing out'. These expressions of 'missing out' and wanting to 'enjoy' being with her child were used by this mother to explain why she gave up work, but the same sentiments were used by some of the part-time working mothers to explain their decision to work part-time hours.

The third mother had worked full time for four months and gave it up because she became increasingly concerned for the safety of her child. Her husband was the main carer (he was unemployed), but she did not trust him and believed his childcare was inadequate. Thus, she said she gave up work 'for the sake of my child'. However, she also gave up because she was unhappy that her job had changed following maternity leave and she was now working with different people whom she disliked.

In essence, all three mothers had been successful in returning to their original jobs after starting a family, but various events acted as catalysts in pushing them to give up work, these included:

- having a miscarriage;
- having a second child;
- believing the childcare was inadequate.

Even so, all three had unsatisfactory job dimensions, including:

- having a stressful job;
- losing their job;
- disliking their job;
- working long days.

Other areas of dissatisfaction were also evident:

- travelling long distances;
- getting 'fed up' juggling childcare and work;
- wanting to 'enjoy' a particular child;
- lacking free childcare for two children.

Having faced the problems outlined above, all three mothers had then decided to postpone returning to work until all their children were in school full time, just like the majority of non-returnees.

Late returnees

For the remaining three mothers who returned to work later after starting a family, there were two points in time where there was a potential to give up work. First, when they may have failed to return to their original jobs following the birth of their first child; and second, when they had to give up the job that they had entered into at a later stage. Each is explored in turn.

Two of the mothers had never returned to their low-skilled jobs following the birth of their first child, one because she wanted to be at home full time with her child, the other because she could not coordinate childcare and work. The problem was that while the grandparents had offered to provide free childcare, the travelling time between the family home, the grandparents' home and the mother's workplace was too great without the use of a car. However, as the mother did not drive and the father was not able to drive them instead (because of his working hours), she was forced to give up her job. The remaining mother had never worked prior to getting pregnant at 16 and had no job to 'return to'. The reasons for not returning included:

- wanting to be a full-time mother;
- never having worked prior to having children;
- coordination problems.

The late returnees therefore had similarities with the non-returnees, where after the birth of their first child they either wanted to be at home or had never worked. Only one late returnee had wanted to go back to work immediately after having her first child, but could not do so because of coordination problems.

Nevertheless, some years later all three late returnees managed to take up part-time unskilled employment. But they only worked in the evenings and relied on grandparents or fathers to provide free childcare. In this regard, they were the same as the part-time working mothers who restricted their employment to atypical hours. However, they only managed to sustain this work for four years in two cases and for six months in the other. They eventually had to give up work because two of them became lone parents and the fathers were no longer able, or perhaps willing, to provide childcare. The other mother was forced to give up work because her hours of employment were changed from evening to daytime and the grandparents could no longer provide childcare as they also worked at these times. All three said they could not consider paying for formal childcare to stay in their jobs as they never earned enough to cover childcare costs. The costs were perceived as being particularly high as both the lone parents had four children and the married mother had three children (all of whom were school/pre-school age). As a result they all decided to postpone returning to work until their children were in school full time.

It seems that the main catalysts forcing these late returnees to give up work included:

- entering lone parenthood;
- changes in the hours of employment.

There was also a common main underlying reason for giving up work:

- losing free childcare provided by fathers or grandparents.

Overall, the main difference between the 12 non-working mothers was that half had returned to work at some point but had given it up, whereas the others had never tried to return to work. Moreover, there were main catalysts driving decisions to give up work, including life-changing events such as having a miscarriage, having more children or becoming a lone parent. Other events included risks to a child's health due to poor quality childcare, or, more mundanely, hours of employment were changed. However, underlying all these catalysts were many other reasons for giving up work and these were related to the nature of the job (too stressful for example) or childcare and coordination issues. Arguably, life-changing events were not sufficient on their own as drivers to giving up work, but became very powerful reasons for doing so when combined with practical problems such as coordination or childcare difficulties. Indeed, the evidence showed that among the working mothers, a few had experienced miscarriages, nearly all of them had a second child, and one mother had become a lone parent, but had continued to stay in full-time employment because she did not rely on her husband for childcare. No single factor was therefore responsible for these non-working mothers having given up work in the past.

Nevertheless, the commonality between non-working mothers was that nearly all of them (bar two) had decided to postpone returning to work until *all* their children were in school. It is possible that postponement is a management strategy in its own right as it allows mothers to be completely self-reliant in managing coordination points. Indeed, it could be a response to perceived coordination problems that were acting as current barriers to return to paid work. It is necessary to probe further into current decisions about paid work and current problems.

Coordination problems in returning to work

Five mothers specifically identified coordination as a current problem in returning to work and this was presented from three main perspectives: first, the inflexible and shifting nature of school nursery hours; or second, the inflexibility of employment to fit around school nursery and/or school hours; or third, transportation issues. Interestingly, the number of children in the family was not presented as a problem, although all five mothers had only one or two children[2].

School nursery provision

In relation to the inflexibility of school nursery provision, one mother who was postponing returning to work said:

"Partly again the childcare is a problem, if I would like [youngest child] to go to nursery [school nursery] it's not flexible enough because he would start in the afternoons, then move to mornings, then he'll move to full days. So fitting something around that sort of criteria over the next three years, which is the point at which he would go to full-time school, is going to be very difficult without somebody to fall back on, maybe to fill a gap." (Mother of two children, one aged four and the other aged 18 months)

This demonstrates the difficulties presented by school nursery. First, the hours are inflexible and shift each term from morning to afternoon or vice versa. This makes it difficult to arrange wrap-around care. Second, the hours are so limited (two-and-a-half hours per day) that it would need to be combined with very flexible private childcare to enable mothers to go to work for any meaningful length of time during the day.

Employment hours

This problem was also identified from an alternative perspective: that of inflexible employment where it would be impossible to find a job to fit around the school nursery and/or school hours. As another mother who was postponing returning to work said:

"How many of us are going to find a job where they can say right, well, for a year I can go afternoons, then I can go part time mornings, and then after that, that six months or whatever, I will be able to come full time for you but still full time where it is something like ten until half past two or

---

2   Having a larger family of three to four children was a factor that influenced mothers' decisions to postpone returning to work, but this was explicitly presented in relation to childcare costs. However, at an implicit level, coordination problems may also have been a factor, but this was not specifically singled out by mothers' with larger families as an issue.

whatever, you know none of us are going
to find a job that fits in [into school nursery
and school hours] like that are we, so."
(Lone mother with two children aged five
and three years)

School nursery provision therefore appeared to
present a current barrier to employment; it was
viewed as problematic in terms of both finding
coordination support to transport children and in
providing wrap-around care to fit in with the
hours of provision. Alternatively, it was viewed
as problematic because it would be difficult to
find flexible enough employment to fit into
school nursery hours. Yet, while this problem is
specifically related to the age of a particular child
(that is, they have to be between three and four
years old to attend school nursery), it also has a
longer time dimension when viewed from a
family perspective. For example, the evidence
showed that where families had more than one
pre-school aged child, the mothers were not only
identifying the current restrictions associated with
having a child in school nursery, but also how
this problem would continue for some years into
the future when their younger children would
start attending. This partly explains why some
mothers were postponing returning to work until
all their children started school. It seems,
therefore, that the ages of children and the age
gap between them, rather than the number of
children in the family per se, were important
factors, especially where age related to part-time
pre-school education.

Transport difficulties

The third perspective on coordination problems
was that of transport difficulties. Two mothers
described transport as problematic because they
could not drive. For example, the mother who
was currently considering returning to work said:

"Then you have got all the logistics,
because I can't drive, of trying to get the
children to these places and then get to
where you have to go you know, if you
can't drive, and obviously [husband] would
not be around to do it because he would
be away working anyway ... yeah for times
of nursery or schools and things and so that
is difficult as well, because it's like trying to
be in a million places at once, and then the
factor of being worn out with it all as well."

(Mother of two children aged four and two
years)

Another mother, a lone parent who also could
not drive, said:

"If you have to catch a bus, you have to
give yourself at least 45 minutes and then
give yourself how many minutes to walk to
work, you are looking at not starting work
until 10 o'clock realistically and then you
have to get back to them when they finish
school at 3 o'clock." (Lone mother of two
children aged five and three years)

What these mothers are describing are the time
restrictions surrounding coordination points and
the difficulties of transporting children and
themselves without the aid of a car. It was
therefore not the inability of mothers to drive
that was the problem, but how a car was needed
in order to successfully condense journey times
at the key coordination points in the day.
Relying on public transport was not a viable
alternative as it elongated journeys, partly
because extra time had to be built in to walk to
the final destination. The consequences of not
being able to condense journey times was
exemplified earlier by the mother who had to
give up her job after having her first child
because she did not have access to a car.
Importantly, it was the time needed to travel a
number of different journeys in a very restricted
time period that was perceived as the real
problem, rather than the distance in miles
(although obviously time and distance are
related). Indeed, both these families were within
10-15 minutes walking distance from the local
primary schools and the two local private
nurseries.

Apart from the three perspectives, another factor
in relation to coordination that was more implicit
was where mothers assumed they had to 'be
there' to collect children from school themselves.

'Being there'

It appeared that 'being there' to collect children
at the post-school coordination point was seen as
an important part of the mother's role or
responsibility. All the non-workers, bar one,
assumed they would have to 'be there' to pick up
children; none of them mentioned AFSCs as an

alternative (even though there were AFSCs in the area). Consequently, they identified how they would have to find employment that dovetailed around the school day, either finishing work prior to the end of school or starting work in the evening post-school. Indeed, this was the work pattern adopted by the majority of the part-time working mothers (13 cases), with seven of them working in the evenings only. However, this latter strategy was unlikely to be so easily adopted among this group of non-working mothers because there were four lone mothers without support from their children's fathers to provide care in the home, and a further five partnered mothers identified this as problematic because the fathers either worked late in the evening or away from home. Nine of the 12 mothers therefore perceived their future choices in returning to work to be very limited indeed. Moreover, the four lone mothers and one of the married mothers also felt their hours of employment would have to be further restricted to term-time only as they had no 'family support' for childcare in the school holidays.

It appears that 'being there' after school stops consideration of AFSCs, as mothers either did not want or did not know about this kind of formal help with the post-school coordination point. It was therefore not necessarily a lack of childcare that acted as a barrier to work here, but mothers' preferences to dovetail their working hours around the school day and in turn the availability of employment that would allow mothers to manage the post-school coordination by themselves. Returning to work in the future therefore depended on surmounting the problem of coordinating work hours with school hours, or altering preferences to 'be there' after school.

Overall, the evidence shows that coordinating school nursery and school hours with work hours is perceived as difficult. This is related to the ages of children in the family; that is, having one child attending school nursery and another at school increases coordination complexity, especially if mothers also want to 'be there' post-school to collect children themselves. This complexity in relation to the ages of children is illustrated most clearly by contrasting the two families in which the mothers were actively looking for a job.

Children's ages and coordinating their needs with work commitments

In the first family (case A-27), this mother was the only one not to discuss 'being there' post-school or to identify coordination as a problem. This is perhaps not surprising as she had only one child aged 18 months. She was now actively looking for a job because she felt that returning to work would be good for her 'psychologically and socially'. However, she said she would only return if it was on her 'own terms'. That meant she would not go back to her original job as it had been too stressful, that she would only work for two days a week and that it had to be 'the right job'. This mother was very clear about what she wanted and she had the luxury of not worrying about money; she stated that she only needed to earn enough to cover her childcare and employment costs. In effect, she was prepared to work for nothing. Thus, coordination was not a problem in this case; first, because their only child of pre-school age was not yet attending school nursery; second, because the mother had access to her own car and presumably would not therefore need support from others with coordination points; and lastly the mother was already using a private nursery two afternoons per week. All that was required was to find the 'right job' to coordinate with her childcare.

In contrast, the mother in the second family (case B-10) who was actively looking for work was consumed with worries about coordination. In this family, there were two children, one child was four years old and was attending school nursery and the other child was two years old. This mother also said that employment would be good for her 'emotionally and socially' and she also wanted added stimulation because she said her 'brains had turned to mush'. Both these mothers therefore expressed very similar reasons for returning to work and they mirror the reasons given by some of the part-time working mothers. However, unlike the first case this mother was very worried about how she would manage coordination points. She worried about trying to be in a 'million places at once' because she could not drive and because her husband worked long hours and he could not help her with picking up and dropping off children. Thus, there was no possibility of arranging informal support with morning and evening coordination points and she worried that she might get 'worn out' as a result. Moreover, she recognised the need for formal support with the lunchtime coordination point; she said she needed a 'very flexible childminder' to both collect her child from school nursery at lunchtime and to be able to adapt her working hours from mornings to afternoons in line with the shifting hours of school nursery. The costs of childcare were also mentioned as a concern, especially as she had to 'pay for two children'. She did, however, have childcare planned in her mind; she had singled out a local registered childminder who she hoped would look after her children. It was not therefore lack of suitable and available childcare or even the costs of childcare that were the overriding factors making her hesitate about returning to work, but coordination complexity. For example, in response to a question about whether childcare costs put her off taking things any further at the moment, she said:

"Umm, cost definitely, but also as I say, it has been up to the dropping off factor because I don't drive, I'm being practical, I probably won't be able to run around all over the place, take one child to nursery and then the other to school, yeah and get on to work you know, so."

It could be that this mother will end up postponing returning to work until *all* her children are in school, especially if she cannot arrange 'flexible childcare' in the form of a childminder to deal with some, if not all, of the coordination points (some of which will change as the school nursery timetable changes).

Summary

This chapter has explored the circumstances of the non-working mothers in this study and shown how these mothers faced fewer coordination points in comparison to working mothers. It also highlighted how some non-working mothers had returned to work in the past but had failed to sustain it due to multiple factors. For example, certain events such as having a miscarriage, having a second child, becoming a lone parent, facing changes in employment hours or having poor quality (family) childcare, acted as catalysts prompting mothers to give up work; although, for many, they had also faced unsatisfactory job

dimensions, such as stressful jobs, disliking their jobs or losing their jobs. Nevertheless, these life events and job problems were simultaneously attached to practical problems in relation to childcare or coordination. The mothers either lost informal childcare because of these events (for example, becoming a lone parent) or the events exposed the difficulties involved in managing coordination (for example, having a miscarriage highlighted to the mother the stress she was enduring in coordinating employment and childcare). Changing life events and circumstances had therefore created interrupted employment histories. However, these events did not fully explain why the majority of these mothers were purposely 'postponing' returning to work until *all* their children were in school.

Further exploration of this concept of 'postponement' highlighted the potential barriers to returning to work in the future, including: the opening times, and the changes in times across terms, of school nursery provision; a lack of efficient transport (public or private) that would allow journey times to be condensed at key coordination points; and the mothers' preferences to 'be there' to collect children from school themselves. It is hard to be certain which of these factors, if any, carried the most weight as a barrier to employment. However, these barriers were more or less surmountable in direct relationship to the ages of children in the family and this was shown most clearly in the comparison made between the two mothers who were actively seeking employment. It appears that, depending on the age of the children in the family, different forms of care/education are needed and this creates greater coordination complexity, which in turn increases the time taken to transport children to and from different care settings. Time costs were increased further if mothers could not condense journey times by either having informal support from fathers and/ or by having an efficient means of transport to manage coordination points. The cost of formal childcare also increased as the number of children in the family increased. However, it seemed that time costs proved to be equally or possibly more important than childcare costs in acting as a barrier in returning to work, particularly where mothers wanted to collect children from school themselves.

The act of 'postponement', therefore, was a management strategy that helped mothers to be self-sufficient and to avoid increasing coordination complexity through taking up paid employment. When all the children were in school the coordination complexity and journey times would presumably reduce, potentially making it easier to return to work. However, these mothers' future work choices still seemed very restricted, first because they wanted to dovetail working hours around the school day so they could 'be there' after school, and second because they could not rely on fathers to provide informal support with coordination points or wrap-around care in the evenings. Either the fathers were non-resident, or they worked long hours into the evening or away from home. Indeed, one of the lone mothers recognised it would be a practical impossibility to return to work under these circumstances, unless she was lucky enough to get a job that matched the school hours but still left her enough time to take the children to and from school herself. However, she recognised that the added problem of not being able to condense journey times (through the use of a car) made working even more unlikely. This demonstrates the important role fathers can play in enabling mothers to return to work. Fathers could provide wrap-around care to help reduce childcare costs and provide informal support with coordination points to help reduce time costs.

6
Conclusion and policy implications

The study reported here did not explore issues surrounding the availability, suitability or quality of childcare provision. Instead, it aimed to explore the everyday experiences among parents from different socioeconomic circumstances in *coordinating* childcare and education for *all* the children in the family alongside work commitments. It also considered whether coordination factors could inhibit maternal employment and whether coordination might be more complex for lower income families.

To reflect varied socioeconomic circumstances, equal numbers of respondents were selected from two different areas; Area A was predominately private market housing and more affluent than Area B, which was mainly social housing. While availability of childcare was not the central focus, the services in the two areas were described in Chapter One. Formal childcare services tended to be fairly centrally located to both Area A and Area B and available to all. Thus, no difficulties were expressed in gaining access. However, access to services was also mediated by parental preferences, and some chose to use services outside the areas (these were mainly parents living in Area A who also had use of a car). This in itself could exacerbate coordination problems, particularly if services were some distance from the family home. In addition, although it might be expected that having greater numbers of children in the family might increase coordination complexity, this was not necessarily the case. Many of those with the most complex arrangements had only two children. However, it is also possible that coordination was such a major problem for families with greater numbers of children (three or more), that the only way to manage children's needs was for the mothers simply not to work. It is hard to be sure from the evidence that this was

the case, as commonly the increased costs of childcare for families with more than two children was cited as the major reason for mothers not working. What seemed very important, however, was that fathers were able to help with transporting children at coordination points, as well as providing wrap-around care. Where fathers were not available (in lone-parent families or where they worked long hours or away from home), then coordination support from others increased and/or became very complex, or mothers (especially lone mothers) felt they could not work. Despite these factors and contrary to expectations, full-time paid work and caring appeared to be the easiest to coordinate, part-time work the most complex and some of the non-working mothers faced so many potential coordination difficulties that it was a disincentive to employment. This aspect of coordinating care, education and employment has not been seriously considered by policy makers and has been given insufficient attention in policy literature.

Coordination management is a complex and skilled activity

A powerful explanatory concept that emerged from the data, 'coordination points', has shown that there is an array of complex, hidden and often precarious management strategies involved in the successful coordination of childcare/education packages with work commitments, including:

- Relying on a network of *informal* and *formal* support to transport children to and from different care settings.

- Arranging *insurance back-up* support in case of a change in routine.

An intimate network of people, including mothers, fathers, family/friends and formal child carers were involved in the daily routine of transporting children safely and efficiently across the settings of home, childcare, school and school nursery education. Given that this sample was biased towards users of formal childcare, this shows a large reliance on informal care, even when formal childcare was also used. Moreover, any changes in routine or unforeseen events had also to be provided for and this often required additional back-up insurance support from family or friends that could involve even more people (see also Mauthner et al, 2001). Thus, the network of support was necessary to ensure that childcare and educational provision were *seamlessly* tied together on a daily basis alongside the parents' work commitments.

It is important to make a distinction here between wrap-around care and seamless care. Wrap-around care refers to provision that is wrapped around parents' working hours and school hours and can be provided formally or informally. However, it cannot be assumed that this is also *seamless care* as the people/ institutions providing wrap-around care may not also collect children from school or pre-school education and take them back to the site in which the wrap-round care takes place. In those circumstances, someone else must be found to transport the children across the school/pre-school and childcare interface. The interface between pre-school education and wrap-around childcare was one of the most problematic to overcome. Some parents went to extraordinary lengths to bridge this gap in order to ensure a seamless service for their children (see case study one). In this regard the local childcare infrastructure was problematic as private nursery day care and public pre-school education were not near to one another or connected.

In order to provide seamless care for children, it was crucial for parents (especially mothers) to manage their network of support along temporal, spatial and time dimensions. The skill required should not be underestimated and is conceivably akin to the tasks involved in project management in an employment setting. Indeed, in order to successfully reconcile paid work, childcare and education, mothers (less so fathers) had to take into account the following factors:

- hours of both parents' employment;
- number of parents available in the household to share coordination tasks;
- availability of childcare/family/friends to help with coordination tasks;
- rules surrounding flexible working practices (if available);
- different times of childcare/educational provision;
- proximity of childcare and educational services to one another and to the family home and workplace;
- availability and efficiency of modes of transport;
- parents' own values about the amount of time a child is cared for by other people;
- parents' own values about the number of people who should be involved in picking up and dropping off children;
- health, developmental and educational needs of children;
- cost of childcare;
- quality and, most importantly, the flexibility of available childcare.

There was also a social dimension as mothers had to negotiate support from family and friends. This seemed most important for the full-time working mothers when arranging back-up support from friends that operated on a reciprocal basis.

Coordination management is about reducing time costs

Underpinning the management of a network of support, some more implicit strategies can be identified where parents were trying to *condense* and/or *accommodate* family journey times at coordination points in order to reduce time costs.

The strategies involved in *condensing* journey times included:

- relying on a fast mode of transport such as a car or even a bike;
- arranging for the different journeys of individual children in the family to occur simultaneously (for example, father/other

transports one child while mother transports another);

- choosing to buy a house in close proximity to school/childcare and/or workplace settings;
- choosing employment in close proximity to the home (mothers tended to exercise this choice);
- choosing childcare in close proximity to the home or workplace.

The strategies involved in *accommodating* journey times included:

- utilising flexitime hours or flexible working hours;
- relying on others to transport children rather than parents doing it themselves;
- choosing working hours to dovetail with school/pre-school education to allow parents to transport children themselves (this usually involved mothers choosing to work atypical hours in the evenings/weekends or working part-time during the day, finishing work prior to the end of the school day);
- choosing to work in a parental shift pattern so that both parents are available at different times of the day to transport children themselves (and in some cases to also allow parents to provide their own wrap-around care).

This is not an exhaustive list, nor are any of the strategies mutually exclusive. All can be used in combination at any one point in time and at different stages in family and working lives. Contradictorily, however, the choices parents made in relation to the quality of childcare provision and/or mothers' working hours could also work in the opposite direction and increase time costs. This was shown most clearly in two cases. In one, the mother chose a private nursery four miles away from the family home and in the other the mother changed her working hours to work shifts, which created an extra coordination point in the evening. As a result, extra support was required with coordination points in both cases. Paradoxically, although flexitime hours were helpful in managing coordination points they also worked to produce greater time costs because the time taken off work to transport children would eventually have to be paid back. Consequently, flexitime hours also created another layer of management as parents had to keep track of debit and credit working hours.

Coordination management is as equally important as service provision

Most importantly, managing coordination was as equally important as childcare provision. For example, the mothers in this study (all of whom had at least one child under five years of age) were successful in sustaining employment because they were able to do one or more of the following:

- Match suitable childcare with employment hours *and* with pre-school educational hours where necessary (for example, either by using flexible childcare if working during the day or by mothers choosing to work in the evenings so they could transport pre-school children to and from education themselves).
- Match suitable childcare with employment hours *and* with school hours (for example, by using an AFSC for school aged children).
- Rely on informal and formal support to accommodate journey times attached to coordination points (or choosing not to work across coordination points so parents could transport children by themselves).
- Manage to condense journey times attached to coordination points by using an efficient means of transport.

These strategies were very complex within themselves. To some extent they were also mediated by parents' 'choices' to work particular hours and their preferences for particular types of childcare and support with coordination points. However, they were unlikely to be easily adopted by the majority of the non-working mothers in the immediate future. Because even if they found suitable childcare, they identified how school nursery provision (which they wanted to use) was particularly problematic. It was only offered for half a day and the time of provision changed from mornings to afternoons across school terms. Thus, the times in which wrap-around care and help with coordination points were needed in order to provide seamless childcare was constantly shifting and it would be difficult to establish any routine support. However, there were also other coordination problems.

The majority of non-working mothers could not accommodate journey times by relying on informal support from fathers with coordination points as fathers were either non-resident, worked away from home or worked long hours. Similarly, because fathers were unavailable to offer wrap-around care, the non-working mothers could not choose to be self-sufficient in transporting children at coordination points by working in the evenings. They also could not accommodate journey times by relying on formal support with coordination points from flexible childminders/nannies as nearly half of them had three or four dependent children and thus childcare would be prohibitively expensive in relation to potential earnings. This suggests it was not the numbers of children in the family per se that increased coordination problems, but how the associated higher childcare costs limited options for formal support with coordination points (and support with childcare).

Many could also not condense journey times by using a car as four were lone parents reliant on Income Support benefit and would be unlikely to afford a car, others could not drive and others did not have access to the 'family car' due to the father's working hours and his dependency on it for his own employment. Public transport was not seen as a viable alternative as it tended to elongate journey times and thus the mother's available time for employment would be reduced. This availability would be reduced even further because mothers believed they should 'be there' to collect the children themselves after school.

Taking these two factors together, that is an inability to either accommodate or to condense journey times, shows that coordination problems alone did not act as a barrier to employment among mothers without access to a car, or to those in the lower income Area B. Nevertheless, having independent access to a car would have helped with managing coordination. In that sense, income level and car access are closely related and therefore both can act as potential factors inhibiting maternal employment, especially where fathers are unable to provide additional support with coordination points.

Thus, for the non-working mothers this was possibly not the right time in their family lives to return to work. The practicalities involved in coordinating childcare and education with perceived work commitments appeared too great to overcome; not least because of the ages of children in the family and their multiple childcare

and educational needs. They also had little option to surmount these difficulties by choosing to work atypical hours because, for many, fathers were not available to provide wrap-around care in the evenings. These difficulties were recognised by the mothers themselves when they described how they were 'postponing' returning to work until *all* their children were in school. Indeed, in only one case was coordination not perceived to be a problem, and that was where the mother had only one child who was also too young for pre-school education. This mother was preparing to return to work if she could find suitable part-time employment. Conceivably, however, as her child grows older and if she goes on to have more children she may find it difficult to sustain this employment without additional support from others with coordination points. Ironically from a policy perspective, this particular mother had no financial need for employment and was prepared to work for nothing after childcare expenses had been paid.

Overall, the concept of coordination points exposes the additional dimensions of time and space that have to be figured into decisions about employment *and* about childcare *and* about education. Considering these additional dimensions has reflected more accurately the real and dynamic nature of reconciling work and family life. Even if parents had suitable childcare, they simply would not be able to do paid work if they could not find an efficient way to transport children at key points in the day that tied in with work commitments, and for that to happen they usually had to rely on support from others. These dimensions of time and space also set some major challenges for policy makers.

Policy implications

The government is promoting labour market participation for mothers and does recognise the need for more childcare places and more flexible employment practices, but less attention has been paid to coordination factors and the need for a better fit between different forms of care to provide seamless provision. Policy makers need to have greater regard for the following factors.

Recognising the gap between early education in a school setting and childcare

In this urban city setting of the study, there was a clear institutional and cultural divide between 'childcare' (in a variety of settings) and 'early education' provided in school nurseries. This created a real spatial and time gap between these two forms of provision. For some mothers this acted as a disincentive in returning to paid work and for other mothers and fathers the arrangements they had in place to bridge the gap were often highly complex and precarious. Although the purpose of early education is not necessarily to provide care to allow parents to go to work, the divide between early education and childcare does seem to be countermanding the intentions within the National Childcare Strategy and the Work–Life Balance Campaign to help parents combine paid work and childrearing.

This is most evident if 'optional early education' is contrasted with 'compulsory school education'. Within compulsory education (where children are generally aged five years or older), the need for 'wrap-around care' and for coordination support to transport children to and from school are recognised as an integral part of AFSC provision. Indeed, without transport help, AFSC provision would be rendered completely useless to working parents as they could hardly be expected to leave work to transport the children themselves. The same could be said then of early education provided within a school setting. This does not facilitate maternal employment, not at least without parents coming up with strategies to bridge the gap between that and childcare. Importantly, the difficulties created by this gap have a longer time dimension when considered from a family perspective. For example, families with more than one child will face the same difficulties as each child reaches school nursery age. This potentially prolongs the time out of the labour market for some women with all the attendant economic disadvantages: interrupted employment histories, reduced earning potential, reduced pension provision, slowing of career progression and loss of employment-based skills. However, the spatial and time dimensions attached to the home and workplace settings have also to be managed for the successful reconciliation of work and family life. This highlights the importance of transport and time costs.

Recognising transport constraints and time costs

This research has shown that parents not only have to arrange suitable and affordable childcare, but they also have to consider the time costs in relation to transporting themselves and children at key coordination points in the day. Parents often used ingenious and complex strategies to accommodate and/or condense these journey times. Flexitime hours were helpful in this regard, but they had a double bind in that time taken off to transport children had to be paid back. This added another layer of management complexity and for full-time working parents it was difficult to pay this time back. Another difficulty for some parents, especially poorer lone parents, was the inefficiency and slowness of public transport, which acted as a barrier to employment. In the UK, there tends to be no specialised transport for children such as school buses (at least in urban settings). The responsibility of transporting children across different care or educational sectors therefore falls completely on the parents. Thus, relying on a car (or in some cases a bike) was a vital part of coordination. Even so, many parents expressed a preference to 'be there' to collect children themselves after school, and it is difficult to know whether extra funding resources put into 'school buses' would be money well spent. However, parental reliance on cars is likely to lead to greater road congestion, further elongating journey times, and this may well have longer term consequences for mothers' employment, for local provision of childcare services and for local transport policy. Indeed, there is some evidence to suggest that transport is already causing problems, as there is a demand for extended childcare opening hours simply to accommodate commuting times. At the same time, however, providers are reluctant to extend childcare hours in the evenings to accommodate these journeys (Statham and Mooney, 2003: forthcoming). Moreover, current transport policies aimed at reducing car use by making it more expensive (for example, congestion charging, charging for workplace parking space) are likely to hit working parents particularly hard.

Recognising the fathers' role in reducing coordination complexity

Many fathers in this study were not only providing wrap-around care but helped in physically transporting children to and from different care settings. Many others were prohibited from doing so because of inflexible employment, long working hours or places of employment far distant from the family home. This presented difficulties for mothers in taking up preferred types of employment, which could be dovetailed around the school day, a preference expressed by the majority in this study and in other surveys (Mauthner et al, 2001; Woodland et al, 2002). Fathers, therefore, played a vital role in facilitating maternal employment in more ways than simply providing childcare. Yet, while fathers' time could be freed up to help with coordination points through improvements in flexible working practices attached to the Work–Life Balance Campaign, the long working hours culture among men and employers in the UK is likely to countermand these efforts.

Overall, the parents in this study used various strategies to deal with the structural and differentiated time and space dimensions of paid work, childcare, pre-school and school education. Taken together these presented formidable challenges to parents in successfully reconciling work and family life. They also present considerable challenges to policy makers *if* they want to recognise the coordination needs of parents and children. Parents have had to adopt strategies to deal with coordination points because, as Moss (2001) has argued, childcare, work and education, and our thinking about them has become compartmentalised and split. More radical ways of thinking about parents' and children's coordination needs are required, including the tackling of the institutional, spatial and cultural divide between education and childcare, the adoption of more effective strategies to deal with the long working hours culture among employers and men in the UK, and the transport needs of children and parents. This gives added weight to the arguments put forward by many that children should be at the heart of policy making and that Children's Centres providing multiple family services should be set up in every neighbourhood and not just in deprived areas (Childcare Commission Report, 2001; Moss, 2001). Notably, plans are being put in place to encourage the integration of public education and private childcare services by making more effective use of school premises within an 'extended schools approach' (Strategy Unit, 2002, p 42). The idea is that schools will become more central to their communities by facilitating the use of their premises to help providers (private and public) supply services such as health, social care and family learning, as well as childcare. However, no specific targets have been set to achieve these plans and it remains voluntary for schools to make effective use of their premises in the ways suggested. Yet, this study shows that working parents are 'running around in circles'; not only are they doing the 'school run', but the 'pre-school nursery run', the 'childcare run' and the 'work run'. The evidence suggests that integrated provision within locally-based schools would help considerably in reducing this coordination complexity; and may minimise some of the barriers to maternal employment.

References

Bertram, T. and Pascal, C. (2001) *Early excellence centre pilot programme annual evaluation report 2000*, DfEE Research Report 258, Nottingham: DfEE Publications.

Blake, M., Finch, S., McKernan, A. and Hinds, K. (2001) *Fourth survey of parents of three and four year old children and their use of early years services (summer 1999 to spring 2000)*, DfEE Research Report RR247, DfEE: Nottingham.

Bryson, C., Budd, T., Lewis, J. and Elam, G. (1999) *Women's attitudes to combining paid work and family life*, London: The Women's Unit.

Callender, C. (2000) *The barriers to childcare provision*, DfEE Research Report RR231, Nottingham: DfEE Publications.

Childcare Commission Report (2001) *Looking to the future for children and families*, London: Kids' Clubs Network.

Crompton, R. (1997) *Women and work in modern Britain*, Oxford: Oxford University Press.

Daycare Trust (2001) Press Release, 29 January.

DETR (Department of the Environment, Transport and the Regions) (2000) *Index of Deprivation 2000*, London: DETR.

Dex, S. (ed) (1999) *Families and the labour market: Trends, pressures and policies*, London: Family Policy Studies Centre.

Dex, S. and Smith, C. (2002) *The nature and pattern of family-friendly employment policies in Britain*, Bristol/York: The Policy Press/ Joseph Rowntree Foundation.

DfEE (Department for Education and Employment) (1998) *Meeting the childcare challenge: Green paper*, London: The Stationery Office.

DfEE (2000) *Changing patterns in a changing world: A discussion document*, Suffolk: Prolog.

DfEE (2001) Press Release, 27 February.

Finch, H. and Gloyer, M. (2000) *Lone parents and childcare: A further look at evaluation data on the New Deal for Lone Parents*, DSS Research Report 68, London: Corporate Document Services.

Glover, H. (1998) *Using ecological concepts to understand balance, work and economic decision-making*, Paper presented to the ESRC seminar series – Parenting, Motherhood and Paid Work, University of Bradford, September.

HM Treasury (2002) *2002 Spending Review, opportunity and security for all: Investing in an enterprising, fairer Britain, new public spending plans 2003-2006*, London: HM Treasury.

Hogarth, T., Hasluck, C. and Pierre, G. with Winterbotham, M. and Vivian, D. (2000) *Work–life balance 2000: Baseline study of work-life balance practices in Great Britain*, Suffolk: Prolog, for the Department for Education and Employment.

Home Office (1998) *Supporting families: A consultation document*, London: The Stationery Office.

La Valle, I., Finch, S., Nove, A. and Lewin, C. (2000) *Parents' demand for childcare*, DfEE Research Report 176, Nottingham: DfEE Publications.

Mauthner, N., McKee, L. and Strell, M. (2001) *Work and family life in rural communities*, York: Joseph Rowntree Foundation.

Moss, P. (2001) 'Where next for 'childcare'?', *Childcare Now*, Issue 14, London: Daycare Trust.

NCOPF (National Council for One Parent Families) (2002) *Lone parents and childcare: The facts*, London: NCOPF.

Paull, G. and Taylor, J. (2002) *Mothers' employment and childcare use in Britain*, London: Institute of Fiscal Studies.

Penn, H. (2000) 'Policy and practice in childcare and nursery education', *Journal of Social Policy*, vol 29, part 1, January, pp 37-54.

Perrons, D. (1998) *Flexible employment and the reconciliation of work and family life*, Paper presented to the ESRC seminar series – Parenting, Motherhood and Paid Work, University of Bradford, September.

Perrons, D. and Hurstfield, J. (1998) *Flexible working and the reconciliation of work and family life or a new form of precariousness*, National report for the UK produced for DGV Economic and Social Affairs Unit, European Commission.

Randall, V. (2000) *The politics of child daycare in Britain*, Oxford: Oxford University Press.

Skinner, C. (2002) 'Childcare provision in the UK', in J. Bradshaw (ed) *The well-being of children in the UK*, London: Save the Children, pp 167-86.

Statham, J. and Mooney, A. (2003: forthcoming) *Around the clock: Childcare services at atypical times*, Bristol/York: The Policy Press/Joseph Rowntree Foundation.

Strategy Unit (2002) *Delivering for children and families: Interdepartmental childcare review – November 2002*, London: Strategy Unit.

Twomey, B. (2002) 'Women in the labour market: results from the spring 2001 LFS', *Labour Market Trends*, March.

Ungerson, C. and Kember, M. (eds) (1997) *Women and social policy: A reader*, Basingstoke: Macmillan Press.

Woodland, S., Miller, M. and Tipping, S. (2002) *Repeat study of parents' demand for childcare*, DfES Research Report 348, Nottingham: DfES Publications.

Appendix A:
Definitions of childcare used in this study

Formal childcare

School nursery = early or pre-school education for children aged between 3 and 4 or 5 years. It is provided free on a part-time basis and attendance is voluntary. Not all primary schools provide nursery education and some private nurseries and playgroups may also provide this service. In this study, where pre-school education was used it was within a primary school setting. During the data collection period for this study, it was offered for half a day and the time of provision changed from mornings to afternoons across school terms. It is hard to be sure how widespread this practice is; it could be common in some areas but not in others.

Nanny = care provided in the child's own home. Care can be provided by resident or non-resident carers, who may or may not be registered with the local authority.

Childminder = care provided generally by a qualified person who has met quality standards and is registered with the local authority (and subject to OFSTED inspection). Care is generally provided in the childminder's own home. In this study, parents' own use of the term 'childminder' was accepted and their childminders may not all have been registered.

Private nursery = fee-paying registered day care for children aged five years or less, usually offered in an institutional setting.

After school clubs = (AFSCs) fee-paying after school care provided mainly by the voluntary/private sector. It is provided as 'wrap-around care' at the end of the school day – from the time school finishes until approximately 6pm. In this study a mix of clubs were used. The two most common clubs used were: first, one within a local community centre in which staff picked up children from the schools and 'walked' them back to the centre; and, second, within a primary school building in which the children were transferred from classroom to the club.

Informal childcare

This is care provided by family (including fathers) and friends/neighbours, and is usually free but is sometimes paid for in kind or in money.

Appendix B:
The European study

As part of a European comparative project entitled 'Welfare and Solidarity in Post-Modern Europe', qualitative research was conducted with 40 parents in five cities across five countries in 1999 (200 interviews). The project was funded by the Danish Social Science Research Council and the Universities of Copenhagen, Roskilde and Umeå. The aim of the project was to use family policies (in relation to paid work and childcare) as a vehicle to describe new models of welfare state regimes. This search for new models would partly be based on experiential data in five countries: Demark, France, Sweden, Germany and England.

The main focus of the empirical part of the project was to explore how families with at least one child under five years of age managed to reconcile work and family life. Specifically, the topic guides in each of the countries explored parents' use of different types of childcare provision (private, public, voluntary and informal), how parents' perceptions of the availability and quality of provision affected decisions about paid work after having a first child and how having a second child affected decisions about childcare provision and about paid work. The European study also explored parents' understanding of the social assistance benefits that provide help with childcare costs. The topic guide was adapted slightly to reflect the UK circumstances. This included a deeper exploration of the questions surrounding who took children to and from different childcare/education settings and the help that parents may have received from others.

The European team aimed to use only summaries of the qualitative interviews for their analysis and to compare this to aggregate statistical data on labour market affiliation (not yet published). Therefore, there has never been a detailed qualitative analysis of the English data. Informed consent was sought from the English respondents for their taped interviews to be stored and made accessible to others for further analysis if required.